I told Ron Padgett that I'd like to have

NICE TO SEE YOU

engraved on my tombstone.

Ron said he thought he'd like to have

OUT TO LUNCH

on his.

—Ted Berrigan

1. Portrait of Ted Berrigan by Alex Katz, 1967. Oil on canvas. Reproduced by permission of Marlborough Gallery.

NICE TO SEE YOU

Homage to Ted Berrigan

Edited and with an Introduction by

ANNE WALDMAN

COFFEE HOUSE PRESS :: MINNEAPOLIS :: 1991

Acknowledgments: The editor wishes to extend special thanks to Alice Notley, Ron Padgett, Sandy Berrigan, Joe Brainard, Jacob Burckhardt, Mark Hillringhouse, Reed Bye, John Waldman, Larry Fagin, Ethie Stearns, Anselm Hollo, Robert Wilson of the Phoenix Bookshop for his help with the checklist, and to Michael Brownstein for the suggestion of the book's title.

The selection by Roberta Bernstein is reprinted from *Jasper Johns' Painting and Sculpture, 1954-1974: "The Changing Focus of the Eye"* by Roberta Bernstein, © 1985, UMI Research Press. Some of the material in this book was originally published in *Exquisite Corpse*, edited by Andrei Codrescu, and used by permission of the editor. "Canzone" by Anne Waldman first appeared in *The Paris Review*. "Desperately Awaiting the Arrival of the China Dinner Man" and "Impatient Poetry for Ted and Alice B." by Philip Whalen are from his book *Heavy Breathing* © 1970, 1971, 1976, 1980, 1983 by Philip Whalen and used by permission of the author. "New York Diary" by Lewis Warsh is from the book *Part of My History* (Coach House Press). "On *The Sonnets*" by Ron Padgett first appeared in the magazine *Brilliant Corners*. "Interview with George Oppen and Ted Berrigan," conducted by Ruth Gruber, first appeared in *Chicago* magazine. "Hearts," "Sonnet XXXVII," "Telegram," "A Religious Experience," "Last Poem," and "As Usual," are excerpted from *So Going Around Cities, New & Selected Poems 1958-1979,* © copyright 1980 by Ted Berrigan. Poems are reprinted here by permission of Blue Wind Press, P.O. Box 7175, Berkeley, CA, 94707.

This project is supported in part by the Dayton Hudson Foundation, with funds from Dayton's and Target Stores. The Publishers thank Morris Golde, Alex and Ada Katz, Kenneth Koch, and Warren Woessner for their donations.

Coffee House Press books are distributed to the trade by Consortium Book Sales and Distribution, 287 East Sixth Street, Saint Paul, Minnesota 55101. Our books are also available through all major library distributors and jobbers, and through most small press distributors, including Bookpeople, Bookslinger, Inland, and Small Press Distribution. For personal orders, catalogs or other information, write to: Coffee House Press, 27 North Fourth Street, Suite 400, Minneapolis, Minnesota 55401.

Library of Congress Cataloging-in-Publication Data
Nice to see you: homage to Ted Berrigan / edited and with an introduction by Anne Waldman.
p. cm.
Includes bibliographical references and index.
ISBN 0-918273-11-0 (alk. paper) : $24.95 — ISBN 0-918273-13-7 (pbk. : alk. paper) : $14.95
1. Berrigan, Ted—Appreciation. 2. Berrigan, Ted, in fiction, drama, poetry, etc. 3. Poets, American—20th century—Biography. 4. American poetry—20th century.
1.Berrigan, Ted. II. Waldman, Anne, 1945- .
PS3552.E74Z79 1991
818' .5409—DC20   90-2696

for Ted's children:

for David

for Anselm & Edmund

&

in memoriam

Kate Berrigan Morrison

1965-1987

"Bon voyage, little ones.

Follow me down
Through the locks. There is no key."

from "In the 51st State" (for Kate)
— Ted Berrigan

Contents

PART THREE

Illustrations

Introduction

ANNE WALDMAN

I never told anyone what I knew. Which is that it wasn't
for anyone else what it was for me.

— from "Cranston Near the City Line"

Edmund Joseph ("Ted") Berrigan was born on November 15, 1934 in Providence, Rhode Island, to Margaret Dugan and Edmund Joseph Berrigan. His father was the chief maintenance engineer at the Ward Baking Company where he designed clever patented innovations for the slicing and baking machinery. According to Ted's sister Kathy Dwyer, it was from their father "Teddy got his intelligence." The family with firstborn Ted and second son Ricky first lived in Cranston:

One clear glass slipper; a slender blue single-rose vase;
one chipped glass Scottie; an eggshell teacup & saucer, tiny,
fragile, but with sturdy handle; a gazelle? the lightest pink flowers
on the teacup, a gold circle, a line really on the saucer; gold
line curving down the handle; glass doors on the cabinet which sat
on the floor & was not too much taller than I; lace doilies? on
the shelves; me serious on the floor, no brother, shiny floor or
shining floor between the flat maroon rug & the glass doors of the cabinet

. . .

There were lilacs in the back yard, & dandelions in the lot.
There was a fence.

— from "Cranston Near the City Line"

They moved to South Providence when Ted was ten years old and Kathy just a year. A third son, Johnny, was to follow. Ted's sister remembers her brother reading a lot, but she never thought him "a real poet" until he moved to New York years later. However, when Ted returned from military service (sixteen months of which were spent in Korea on sentry duty, drinking beer, seeing little action and visiting Japan) in 1957 and lived on the top floor of the three-story house in which the family rented rooms, his sister can remember straightening up his books and papers, and removing empty Pepsi bottles which were "everywhere and under the bed." She also remembers a record player continually playing The Weavers. "Teddy was the kind who talks to you as the person you are. Even after he'd moved to New York City, when he came home it was as if he'd never changed. He didn't put on airs. He was the older brother, dutiful son, interested in little things around the house, local gossip. He was interested in you." This quality of sincere attention which his sister describes was characteristic of Ted throughout his life. He had a persistent and compulsive interest in the world, a love affair with *other.*

He often seemed to know and care more about his friends and colleagues than they did about themselves. This attention could be inspiring, saintly, nurturing, meddlesome, maddening. His perceptions and repartee were frequently so brilliant, scathing and fast that they created a pressurized situation that before his company knew it drew them irresistibly into "Ted's world." He was a father-confessor, elder-poet-teacher, the one to whom younger writers wanted to show their new work. He could be a devastating or elevating critic. When Ted died in 1983, more than one young poet was heard lamenting that now Ted wouldn't be there to read his (the young poet's) poems anymore! Ted became a dominating presence in many people's lives because he made the

2. Ted Berrigan in Korea, circa 1954.

world more cohesively scenic, dramatic and funny and included everyone in this vibrant world. He loved details and how people said things. He lit up at an awkward phrase. He enjoyed energy and rigor in intonation and speech. His ear was as quick as his tongue.

Ted had attended Providence College before entering the army, and after his stay in Providence following the Korean War, he went to the University of Tulsa on the G.I. Bill, completing a B.A. and working on his Master's thesis: *George Bernard Shaw: The Problem of How to Live.*

3. Ted Berrigan at the University of Tulsa, circa 1958. Yearbook photograph.

4. Ted Berrigan & Dick Gallup, Providence, Rhode Island, February 1961. Photograph by Ron Padgett.

He was also in the National Guard, finishing his military service and according to Ron Padgett had some "marching duties" on weekends. In Tulsa he had met Ron, Joe Brainard and Dick Gallup, and the four constituted what John Ashbery later humorously referred to as the "soi-disant Tulsa School." They rendezvoused in New York City in 1960-61, along with Pat Mitchell, who had also attended the University of Tulsa. Pat Mitchell and Ron Padgett were married in 1963.

When Ted finally completed his thesis in New York in 1962, he received his Master of Arts certificate in the mail, but being the serious, modest poet he was, he sent it back with the note "I am the Master of No Art."

HEARTS

At last I'm a real poet I've written a
ballade a sonnet a poem in spontaneous
prose and even a personal poem I can use
punctuation or not and it doesn't even
matter I'm obscure when I feel like it
especially in my dream poems which I never even
call Dream Poem but from sheer cussedness title
Match Game Etc. (for Dick Gallup) or something like that.

For example, take this poem, I don't know how
to end it, It needs six lines to make it a sonnet, I
could just forget it and play hearts with Joe and
Pat and Dick, but lately I'm always lethargic,
and I don't even like hearts, or Pat, or Joe, or
Dick or/and especially myself, & this is no help.

In 1962 Ted was visiting Dick Gallup, who was then attending Tulane University in New Orleans, and through him met Sandra Alper from Florida, a student at Sophie Newcomb College. After an intense weekend courtship Ted and Sandy got married, with considerable resistance from Sandy's horrified parents who considered Ted an unfit and dangerous consort:

I never thought
on the Williamsburg Bridge I'd come so much to Brooklyn
just to see lawyers and cops who don't even carry guns
taking my wife away and bringing her back
— from "Personal Poem #9"

A son, David, was born to Sandy and Ted in 1963. Ted was also writing his innovative poem sequence, *The Sonnets*, that same year, and editing *"C"* Magazine and Press.

SONNET XXXVII

It is night. You are asleep. And beautiful tears
Have blossomed in my eyes. Guillaume Apollinaire is dead.
The big green day today is singing to itself
A vast orange library of dreams, dreams
Dressed in newspaper, wan as pale thighs
Making vast apple strides towards "The Poems."
"The Poems" is not a dream. It is night. You
Are asleep. Vast orange libraries of dreams
Stir inside "The Poems." On the dirt-covered ground
Crystal tears drench the ground. Vast orange dreams
Are unclenched. It is night. Songs have blossomed
In the pale crystal library of tears. You
Are asleep. A lovely light is singing to itself,
In "The Poems," in my eyes, in the line "Guillaume
        Apollinaire is dead."

5. Ted Berrigan with Kate Berrigan, in New York City. Photograph by Lorenz Gude, circa 1965.

A daughter, Kate, was born in 1965. The following year The Poetry Project at St. Mark's Church In-the-Bowery began where Ted served on the advisory committee and led a writing workshop, his first official teaching post. The workshop was a great success and Ted taught on and off at The Poetry Project until 1979. His presence at the Wednesday Night Readings always enhanced and enlivened the proceedings. Once when the plane carrying John Wieners to New York from Boston for a reading at St. Mark's was delayed, Ted started up a football game to keep everyone busy and amused. He was a most compassionate "bouncer" and reasoned patiently and convincingly with the belligerent stray or drunk who reeled into the Parish Hall.

6. Ted Berrigan teaching at the University of Iowa, 1968.

In 1968 Ted left New York City to take a writer-in-residence position at The University of Iowa Writers' Workshop. This was the beginning of a peripatetic teaching career that would take him to the University of Michigan in Ann Arbor, Yale University, The State University of New York at Buffalo, Northeastern Illinois University, The University of Essex in England, The Naropa Institute in Boulder, Colorado, Stevens Institute of Technology in Hoboken and finally, at the end of his life, The City College of New York. Wherever he went he transformed the lives and writing of his students, inviting them to join the ever-widening circle of poets, artists and friends based for the most part in New York's Lower East Side.

> Big Town will wear you down
> But it's only here you can turn around 360 degrees
> And everything is clear from here at the center
> To every point along the circle of horizon
> Here you can see for miles & miles & miles
> Be born again daily, die nightly for a change of style
> Hear clearly here; see with affection; bleakly cultivate compassion
> Whitman's walk unchanged after its fashion.
> —from "Whitman in Black"

If Ted's disciples were serious about making poems and interested in artistic "community," they invariably arrived on the Lower East Side where Ted held court, monitoring the cultural, aesthetic and social affairs of the day. Many former students and friends picked up the mannerisms of Ted's speech and poetry, and moved in their own ways from there. Ted's opinions, his "takes," rippled out into the community and carried a political influence within this extended family. His teaching was personal and absolute, tough and tender and full of zest for life and literature. He told his Naropa students to read a book a day, *at least*.

In 1971 Ted married poet Alice Notley who had been a graduate student at the Iowa Writers' Workshop. They had two sons, Anselm, born in 1972, and Edmund, born in 1974. The family was remarkable for its simultaneous intimacy and openness.

> Anselm is sleeping; Edmund is feverish, and
> Chatting; Alice doing the *Times* Crossword Puzzle:
> I, having bathed, am pinned, nude, to the bed
> Between Green Hills of Africa &
> The Pro Football Mystique. Steam is hissing
> In the pipes, cold air blowing across my legs . . .
> Tobacco smoke is rising up my nose, as Significance
> Crackles & leaps about inside my nightly no-mind.
> — from "Small Role Felicity"

Ted's death in 1983 at age 48 followed years of difficult health problems, compounded by amphetamine use, but was nevertheless a tremendous shock to all of us who had grown to assume that "the world contained Ted." He was stubborn, and resistant to doctors. It was as if he were too many people for his ailing body. At the Jack Kerouac Conference in Boulder in the summer of 1982 he told me he was dying. He pronounced this as fated. He wasn't asking for help or sympathy particularly, but wanted me to understand why he'd have to miss a class, why his energy was lagging. He was usually private about his illnesses and would simply shut the door that was otherwise always open. His eldest son, David, then a serious biology student at Reed College in Oregon, was visiting and wound up taking care of him in Boulder.

Looking back at the poems, one can now see how he was preoccupied with his own death:

TELEGRAM

    to Jack Kerouac

Bye Bye, Jack.
 See you soon.

      ★

The end
Came quickly & completely without pain, one quiet night as I
Was sitting, writing, next to you in bed
                          —from "Last Poem"

In 1979 he wrote:

I am 43. When will I die? I will never die, I will live
To be 110 & I will never go away, & you will never escape from me
    who am always & only a ghost, despite this frame, Spirit
Who lives only to nag.
I'm only pronouns, & I am all of them, & I didn't ask for this
    You did
I came into your life to change it & it did so & now nothing
    will ever change
That, and that's that.
Alone & crowded, unhappy fate, nevertheless
    I slip softly into the air
The world's furious song flows through my costume.
                          —from "Red Shift"

In a resumé compiled October 31, 1982, Ted wrote of himself under General Description: "mostly venerable, large, traditional in appearance." Then under Remarks, he added: "Formidable, affable, durable, currently somewhat available."

He was definitely all these things to his many friends. Always the consummate American of expansive Irish Catholic extraction, working class, Korean vet, husband, father, lover, a rebel who ate white bread and sugared donuts and scoffed at anything green ("Green noodles for supper again, Anne?"). He died appropriately on July 4, 1983, and was buried at Calverton National Cemetery in Long Island with an American flag draped over his coffin. The coffin looked a good deal smaller than Ted, and at the funeral Ed Sanders and I mused about whether he could really be in there.

This Homage presents reminiscences by many of the poets and artists who were Ted's friends, as well as selected interviews, poems, letters, critiques, comics, photographs and collaborations covering a span of nearly twenty-five years. As such, it is a slice of recent American poetical history, both personal and urban-cultural, as well as a salute to the life and work of Ted Berrigan by those who loved him and learned much about poetry and generosity from him.

> I open a beautiful letter
> from you. When we are both dead,
> that letter
> will be Part Two
> of this poem.
> — from "Today in Ann Arbor"

> — Anne Waldman
> The Jack Kerouac School of
> Disembodied Poetics
> The Naropa Institute
> Boulder, Colorado, July 1986.

PART ONE

Sonnet LXXVII

"Dear Chris

it is 3:17 A.M. in New York city, yes, it is
1962, it is the year of parrot fever. In
Brandenburg, and by the granite gates, the
old come-all-ye's streel into the streets. Yes, it is now,
the season of delight. I am writing to you to say that
I have gone mad. Now I am sowing the seeds which shall,
when ripe, master the day, and
portion out the night. Be watching for me when blood
flows down the streets. Pineapples are a sign
that I am coming. My darling, it is nearly time. Dress
the snowman in the Easter sonnet we made for him
when scissors were in style. For now, goodbye, and
all my love,
    The Snake."

— *Ted Berrigan*

Letter to Sandra Alper Berrigan

TED BERRIGAN

Sunday afternoon on the east side of New York and out the window kids are playing on a giant fifty-foot mound of sand in a building area. I want to go play too. I wish you were here. I wish, I wish you were here,

Dear Sandy

I found a picture of a beatnik today in a history book. What do you think?

He's the captain of the *Monitor* which fought the *Merrimac* in the first battle between armored ships. Probably wrote his poetry between battles or during. (He must be a poet, look at his hair and beard. Probably was a horrible narcotics addict too.)

I wish I knew what a beatnik was so I could be one.

I've written three poems in the three days I've been here. O happy New York. And all the time I feel you. My writing is new, and better, and I know it's because of love. Which means you.

Last night I saw a bad opera based on Goethe's story *The Sorrows of Werther*. Do you know it? It's the story of a tragic love ending in suicide. The opera was bad, but Goethe is great. Werther was the first romantic, or something like that. These days though, we who feel who live who love romance understand it through John Wayne's eyes. Which is good. (What am I saying?) I'm not really incoherent. I'm in a kind of trance from reading Henry Miller's *Tropic of Capricorn*. It is so great I have to stop every few pages and wonder. After speaking of killing birds to eat (a fantasy) he writes:

> If I killed a little bird and roasted it over the fire and ate it, it was not because I was hungry but because I wanted to know about Timbuctoo or Tierra del Fuego. I had to stand in the vacant lot and eat dead birds in order to create a desire for that bright land which later I would inhabit alone and people with nostalgia. I expected ultimate things of this place but I was deplorably deceived. I went as far as one could go in a state of complete deadness, and then by a law, which must be the law of creation, I suppose, I suddenly flared up and began to live inexhaustibly, like a star whose light is unquenchable.

Sandy, my beautiful, innocent wife, Miller has just said simply much of what I have been struggling to tell you. If I eat dead birds in vacant lots, it is not because I am hungry, but because I need to discover Tierra del Fuego, the land

7. *Portrait of Sandy* by Joe Brainard, 1963. Mixed media collage.

of fire, the fiery earth. I people my poems with nostalgia. They are in part my bright land. And through the past few months, and most of all through loving you, through marrying my soul, my self to yours as was preordained, I have now flared up like a burning rose, like a dove, and begun to live inexhaustibly, like a star whose light is unquenchable, good to eat a thousand years. Thank you.

I send you this picture of a man. The faces of saints shine with a light that reveals them to you, and to me, and to whomever has eyes to see.

Camus has been dead for two years. Dead at mid-life.

Tonight Dick and I and Joe are going to *Breathless* and *L'Avventura* in a double bill. You and I will see them again when you are here. *Breathless* is so frantic, so nervous, so controlled anyway. So alive. *L'Avventura* is like a dying life. Days take minutes. Seconds sometimes last for hours. In both pictures, from opposite sides of the coin, marvelous things are done with time. To rip out of the mind of human beings the dead concept of time as mathematical . . . time is not arithmetical. Nor is it geometrical. It is magic. It is unexplainable, like the force of life, the élan vital, the primal drives. The revolutions of the earth deceive us. Time is Space is Life. Einstein is the supreme poet. Korzybski is his prophet. Bergson and Whitehead went to the desert, and came back to show us the way: where? to our own desert, so we could find our own way. Everyone does everything himself. All those who are going to make it will, all those who aren't won't. Miller writes:

> And now here I am, sailing down the river (life) in my own little canoe. Anything you would like to have me do for you I will do — gratis. In this land, the bright land, the spermatazoon reigns supreme. Nothing is determined in advance, the future is absolutely uncertain, the past is nonexistent. For every million born, 999,999 are doomed to die and never again be born. But the one that makes a home run is assured of life eternal. Life is squeezed into a seed, which is a soul. Everything has soul, including minerals, plants, lakes, mountains, rocks. Everything is sentient, even the lowest stage of consciousness. Once this fact is grasped, there can be no more despair. At the very bottom of the ladder, chez the spermatazoa, there is the same condition of bliss as at the top, chez God. The river starts somewhere in the mountains and flows on into the sea. On this river which leads to God the canoe is as serviceable as the dreadnought. From the very start the journey is homeward.

Honey, keep faith. They can't touch you, us, after all.

I'm waiting, waiting to hear from you, to hear what is going on, what is happening, what is going to happen. I am at an impasse, because I can do nothing until I hear from you, or your doctor, or your parents. I have no money, only New York, and Dick and Joe and always and ever our love. And because of that this life is all good. The hospital, your mother and father, the deputies, the Negro clerk at the Norfolk Hotel, the private detectives, the people outside I have not met yet, it's all somehow good in spite of itself. We have love, you and me, and that makes even separation be good. To be together is the same as to be separate when there is love that is love. No one can touch that love. We are never apart. I am with you, you are here, even when we are not thinking of each other. Love is before thought, beyond thought. No one can understand that we ran off after five days. How can we expect them to understand that we loved each other before we even met? I loved you in Pat, and in Anne Kepler and in Dick, and Dave Bearden and Jim Sears, and in my mother, and in Rilke and Whitman and Mozart and Harpo Marx. You knew me as Dick and as Lenny, and as Leslie, as your father, as Stone, and Doris, and Antoine St. Exupery, as Ed Kaim, and as Hayakawa, and John Wayne, and Khatchatchurian. When we met we knew each other, had known each other for a million years. When you feel pangs for Lenny, it is because he is me, and I am him, and yet we are two different husks of body and to have one seems to be to lose the other. But it isn't to lose other. I love him because he knew to look at you. My small mind may be jealous, but the me that is me knows that we are all one another and one soul. I love you, because to me you are everything, everybody, the world. And I must love the world if I love you. You are the best of everything, the good that is in everything. My sweet, my dear, we, the world, are all in love with you.

—Ted Berrigan
1962

Letter to James Schuyler

TED BERRIGAN

Dear Jimmy,

Just a note. I hope you've gotten the latest *"C"* by now. We are sending them out a few at a time for lack of stamp money. But if it hasn't arrived it should soon. I'm putting together *"C"* number 7 now, and hope to get it out in three weeks. I'm tremendously impressed with it so far, and "The Home Book" is the prize piece among poems by Frank O'Hara and Kenneth Koch, your and Kenward's play, John Ashbery's note on Andy Warhol, a poem by John Wieners, and some things by Ron Padgett, Dick Gallup and myself. I've tentatively decided to use two poems by you besides "The Home Book," the sonnet beginning, "August, smelling of ripe grapes and afternoon sleep," and

8. Ted Berrigan and Ron Padgett, circa 1963. Photograph by Lorenz Gude.

the one beginning, "In the cafe I sat and watched the rain."

I want to use the others I have by you in future issues, and I'm waiting eagerly for the other poems you spoke about in your letter.

What a good writer you are! Ron and I found two copies of *Alfred and Guinevere* in a used book store the other day, and immediately bought them, and I've been rereading them, as well as a copy of your poem "December." I'm just dazzled by the graceful quality of your writing!

Frank O'Hara said that I should be sure and ask you about a story you have, whose name he couldn't recall, that he said was about two homosexuals named Clyde and Henry . . . do you know the one he means? He said it was a marvelous story and that he knew I'd love it. Also (it seems that your manuscripts circulate just like Elizabethan court sonnets) John Button says he has a play by you called, I think, *February* which may not have been published. It's so interesting and great that on the few occasions when I see people like John and Frank and Kenward and some others, whenever your name comes up everyone has lots of things of yours in mind that they think are great and should be published immediately! Your work makes up an "underground movement" all by itself!

Anyway, I hope you can send some more poems soon, or prose or plays or anything. And I hope we can meet. I don't know if I can ever get out to Southhampton, although I want to get out to Keene's bookstore sometime to get a copy of *Meditations in an Emergency* which can't be gotten here, but if I get a chance to do that I'd like to call first and see if you're going to be free.

All Wishes,
Ted
January 30, 1964

On *The Sonnets*

RON PADGETT

For years now, since the early sixties at least, Ted Berrigan has kept a journal, where he probably made notes about the writing of *The Sonnets*. My memory of those details is hazy. Apparently the first sonnets were written in the winter and spring of 1963.

Ted was twenty-nine. The previous several years had seen him take up amphetamine; move to New York; become involved with several young women; write his Master's thesis on George Bernard Shaw; return his M.A. certificate with the note, "Keep this, I am the master of no art"; live on the down and out, mostly by writing papers for students at Columbia, by bumming money from his friends, and by stealing, reading, and reselling the books he could not buy — an incredible number of those; striding at top speed from one movie theater, art gallery, and museum to another; drinking gallons of coffee and yakking all night and into the next day; hopping in a car, driving to New Orleans, marrying a girl he'd just met, spiriting her away from the Florida mental institution where her horrified parents had her incarcerated for such an impulsive marriage to such a dubious character, and going on the lam with her to Denver; and finally returning to the City, to a rented room on 113th Street between Broadway and Amsterdam.

In this room, with his young wife, his books, his records, his manuscripts, and his pills, he began the sonnets, the first four or five in one night, as I recall; then a chunk of three or four more, then more; and Ted, I believe, had to hold his breath: *he was on to something.* It was like a dream in which you find a suitcase that is filled with money, each bill a hundred, no! a thousand dollars. You can't believe your luck and the feeling sweeping over you! Ted seems to have sustained that magic moment throughout the writing of *The Sonnets,* which took only a few months.

In a sense, some of *The Sonnets* had already been written. Many of the lines he used were from previous poems of his, or from translations or mistranslations he'd done. Some were entire poems he had written as far back as the fall of 1961 — "Personal Poem #2" became "Sonnet LXXVI." Some lines were "lifted" out of poems by John Ashbery, Kenneth Koch, and Frank O'Hara, or from Ted's immediate friends, such as Dick Gallup, Joe Brainard, and me. It was of course not a question of plagiarization — a term that sent us into spasms of laughter—it was a matter of using "found" lines to create an entirely different work, and the intentions were, if I may use such a word here, noble.

Ted had a license to operate in this no-holds-barred manner, a license granted by Duchamp, Tzara, Arp, and Ernst (and later, Burroughs); particularly Duchamp, who was like a god to us. The heroic example of Abstract Expressionism (especially de Kooning, Pollock, and Hans Hofmann) was constantly before us, with each day big and exciting and "all-over." And—to help tie it all together—hadn't Frank O'Hara written a book on Pollock?

Anyway, at that time we didn't speak English, we spoke Poetry. Our conversation was studded with quotations from the poetry we idolized. If a supermarket were closing, we'd point and laugh and say, "The academy of the hamburger is closing its doors" (a variation on a John Ashbery line), or we'd say hello with something such as "I see you are wearing your pink Francis Picabia diapers today!" (a travesty of Kenneth Koch). Such pseudo-quotations ran from these contemporaries back to Stevens, Pound, Williams, Rimbaud, Conrad Aiken, and others (Shakespeare, Homer, Virgil, and Dante). Ray Charles, Miguel Aceves Mejia, Leadbelly, Woody Guthrie, Cisco Houston, Big Bill Broonzy, Eric Darling, our Caedmon records of modern poetry—especially Stevens' "Idea of Order at Key West," with its sibilance and stateliness and mysterious "sacred portals dimly starred"—and our Oscar Williams anthologies, these were all literally worn out in a period of several years, as Kerouac's and Ginsberg's books had been a few years before. We had become living anthologies of literature, striding, excited and harmlessly obnoxious, through the streets of New York rejoicing!

This does not explain, though, why *The Sonnets* were written—or rather built—when they were. My guess is that you can expand only so far without being blown to pieces, and that it was time for Ted to consolidate. It is easy to point out the variousness of tones and influences in this work, less easy to describe the craftsmanship involved. I said "built" rather than "written" because, as Ted himself has said several hundred times, he was using words as though they were bricks he placed side by side, one course after another, tapping them into place with his old typewriter that required a firm wham of the fingers. Scissors and Elmer's glue were also essential tools.

Not a single poem in *The Sonnets* conforms to the classical definition of the sonnet, either Shakespearean or Italian, and yet the sense of the sonnet, the feel of the well-crafted "little song," hovers behind them all. Ted had written imitations of Shakespeare's sonnets a couple of years before. The changes he rung on the traditional sonnet form, with a good dose of the hypnotic repetition

of lines in the pantoum form, are particularly interesting. The line enjamb-
ments, the twisting of syntax, the "push-pull" of meaning, the abrupt changes
of tone, the dislocation of punctuation, the fading in and out of prosody, the
intentional misuse of parts of speech, the aesthetic decisions as to when to accept
the results of a chance operation or to discard them—these should not be
overlooked in favor of colorful subject matter.

For personal reasons I wasn't seeing very much of Ted while he was writing
The Sonnets, though we lived nearby and had the same friends. But by late spring
of 1963, when he started *"C"* magazine, I was feeling friendlier, and by the
spring of 1964 he had started publishing *"C"* Books. He edited my first
collection and I edited the first edition of *The Sonnets,* four hundred copies with
a beautiful cover by Joe Brainard, to whom the book is dedicated. Actually
there was very little editing as such on either side. He produced what I wanted
in my book and I produced what he wanted in his. I remember typing the
mimeograph stencils and marvelling at the poems and marvelling at how I was
seeing them in a way you can't see them unless you actually sit down and type
them, almost as though you were writing them yourself.

A few years later Donald Allen at Grove Press published a new edition of
The Sonnets which went through two printings (6,000 copies) and is now out of
print. Temporarily, I am sure.★ Because, unlike so many poems Ted and I wrote
in the early sixties, and despite moments of sentimentality and self-importance,
The Sonnets have held up, because the art is good. They *are* feminine, they *are*
marvelous, they *are* tough.

—Ron Padgett
December 1978

★ *The Sonnets* was reprinted by United Artists, NYC in 1982. (Ed.)

At the Poetry Conference: Berkeley After the New York Style

ROBERT DUNCAN

I.
Beginning with sonnets for Ted Berrigan
Turning on poetry and I'm off
Along lines Ginsberg is reading to places
It takes a line in here I have not heard
Beautiful yellow cheeks and jowls

Marking an uneven stanza off with jewels
Little girls reading all the way thru 88
Highway into some part of Oregon
Goddess of music and poetry by-pass
Where Allen Ginsberg says *"This"*
A line for you in your own collection
It is eight forty-five and two more

For closing we need something lovely
That will lead on to closing doors we see.

2.
Same evening. Can anybody.
Turning on poetry I have not heard
Ham it up so and still get down
From there he takes O'Hara
Who never really went there
where he did not come.   From.   They said.

He did little girls reading all

This one in a Black Mountain
Berrigan imitation North Carolina
Lovely needed poem for O'Hara
and Ashbery again going towards the Pound

Cantos with ashes and berries for the
Contempt they feel and gratitude and
for the puns sake
Dogs barking along another shore.

You never gave me my road.
What could I do for *you*?

3.
They are crowding in the doors to hear
Ginsberg. But Duncan
Is writing Sonnets from the Portuguese
For T. Berrigan with run-on
Effusions of love and lines in rime
(Which I have to postpone until later)

Allen is saying various things amusing.
I am singing Kenneth Koch even might be here
If they were written by John Ashbery
So turned on by Berrigan going off
towards uptown

He didn't know I wrote the song
I have choruses of the West sing
Cantos and for Pound's sake
Envoys and aves buses can have.

Byron Keats and Shelley are our boys abroad.
Sketch of a vista confronting the ocean.

4.
Dear familiar words *"cock"* and *"cunt"*
(Ginsberg is unbeknownst to Far Rockaway
Where in 1941 I went to meet Anaïs Nin
But it was raining and February.
Frank O'Hara was probably in school.
Now at my most lovely

Never having been to Harvard for God's sake
I'd like to make up a life of my own
Berrigan can have from me to think over.

Dear familiar words like . . . But no
Words come (I'm so shy when words are familiar
"Fate passing by" Allen is bellowing
Nor was I unhappy.   How much I love to be made love to
By delicate girl-hands
The whole thing belonging to Berrigan.

5.
An old creep with a need to read poems
Has only my sonnets to Berrigan to read
So I put in the word *"Jack Off"* from Ginsberg's mouth
A line for you in your own collection.
We let the river run if it wants to.

Dogs barking along the other shore.
I put the coda towards the last
for friendship's sake
Envoys and buses O'Hara needed
To get where I am behind times and scenes
[Do this passage in a BIG VOICE]

The audience is crowding in
To hear what we need and is lovely.

                                        —Robert Duncan
                                        1965

After the Sonnets

CLARK COOLIDGE

Absence of trees, medallions like best caps
love is adrift, a night without lurking
In the wheat arena, a portion of sorrow
milked like a duck, his eyes go straight
And in snow, Pontchartrain is missed, keys
thought wrong are hit, a penny for all your dialing
But stored up, love, then let off this time
dwindlers in rows, the main portion silent
That I keep telling but you, the ace of this
fritillary map fob, ruling sign: cabbages
No noise please fret, sumps to be drilled and
poems hoist, do you freight me in this?
My keen knock the pencil makes tracks for
this bound hand, why can I write for my mind can't?
Strong bands thrill the police, even as cars
cancelling, sundown, labor and eggs
Of my eyes make, when love has your hold on
masked signs, but masked eyes do see

December 18, 1981

From *Jasper Johns' Paintings and Sculptures, 1954-1974*: "The Changing Focus of the Eye"

ROBERTA BERNSTEIN

Near the upper left corner of *Screen Piece 3,* Johns silkscreened the title page and adjoining blank page of a book of poems by Ted Berrigan, *The Sonnets* (1964). There are many aspects of *The Sonnets* which would have appealed to Johns at this time, but I think the most important was the way the poems were conceived as a series. They are all written in the sonnet form and certain lines reappear in different poems, sometimes fragmented or slightly altered. Two of the poems, "Penn Station" and Sonnet XXI, are made up of identical lines rearranged. Johns' *Screen Pieces* are likewise the same format, and contain motifs which are repeated in each version. Johns was reading *The Sonnets* in November 1967, when he was beginning work on his *Screen Pieces,* and I think these poems reaffirmed or possibly inspired the idea of a closely related series of paintings.

Another feature of Berrigan's poems relevant to the *Screen Pieces* and other of Johns' works, is their collage effect. Lines seem to be fragments of thoughts, remembrances, or images juxtaposed seemingly at random, for example, Sonnet XV:

> In Joe Brainard's collage its white arrow
> He is not in it, the hungry dead doctor.
> Of Marilyn Monroe, her white teeth white-
> I am truly horribly upset because Marilyn
> and ate King Kong popcorn, he wrote in his
> of glass in Joe Brainard's collage
> Doctor, but they say "I LOVE YOU"
> and the sonnet is not dead.
> takes the eyes away from the gray words,
> Diary. The black heart beside the fifteen pieces
> Monroe died, so I went to a matinee B-movie
> washed by Joe's throbbing hands. "Today
> What is in it is sixteen ripped pictures
> does not point to William Carlos Williams.

This poem makes sense when the first and last lines are read in sequence, then the second and second to the last, etc. Johns was reading Sonnet XV when I visited him one evening in November 1967 at the Chelsea Hotel where he was

9. *Screen Piece 3* by Jasper Johns, 1968. The title page of the Grove Press edition of *The Sonnets* is in the upper left-hand corner. Photo by Eric Pollitzer.

living at the time. He had just discovered this order and read the poem to me. He then read other poems from Berrigan's *Sonnets,* choosing favorite lines, several of which I cite below.

There are reflections on the creative process in *The Sonnets,* which are thematically relevant to Johns' art: e.g. "Everything turns into writing / I strain to gather my absurdities into a symbol" (XLV); "(cleave to a cast-off emotion — Clarity! Clarity!)" (LXXI); "I'll break / My staff bury it certain fathoms in the earth / And deeper than did ever plummet sound / I'll drown my book." (LXXXVIII). There are references to art, like "Harum-scarum haze on the Pollock streets" (XIX); allusions to Duchamp which have the same cryptic quality as Johns' Duchamp references: "A man / Breaks his arm so he sleeps he digs / In sleep half silence and with reason" (XXXVIII); "in advance of the broken arm" (XLI); "Signs a shovel and so he digs" (LXXXVIII). Gertrude Stein, one of Johns' favorite authors, is mentioned in the following line: "for everything comes to it / gratuitously like Gertrude Stein to Radcliffe" (LII). Sonnet LV is dedicated to Frank O'Hara; the first line is a quote from his poem, "In Memory of My Feelings": "Grace to be born and live as variously as possible." In Berrigan's poems, as in O'Hara's, there are many references to friends, lovers and autobiographical events. Alluding to particular poets and poems, even through a name or title only, enabled Johns to bring personal associations and feelings into his own work indirectly through the intermediary of poetry.

—Roberta Bernstein

From *Program Report from 80 Langton Street, San Francisco Writer in Residence :: Ted Berrigan :: June 24-27, 1981*

RENNY PRITIKIN

When Ted Berrigan took the rostrum to begin his four-day residency at 80 Langton this past June, it was the actual start of an event that had already been taking place psychologically for some time, given all the anticipation, excitement, rumor and resentment that only the arrival of a major figure can engender. This first and the final, fourth night were reserved for readings by Berrigan, a well-conceived bracketing of the residence, a gesture reiterating the primacy of the work amid the flurry of official and unofficial conversation about to ensue. However, a definitive accomplishment of 80 Langton's series of residences has been the public interchange among serious working writers about issues in their work. Berrigan's ambivalence about this element of the series was not the only thing soon apparent. His informal yet highly revealing introduction to the first public reading of the entire *Sonnets* became a microcosm of the residence and perhaps Berrigan's esthetic approach in general. Rather than the straight-forward, clearly stated goals, interest and principles that the Langton audience has come to expect from many residents, it became apparent that Ted Berrigan didn't care to articulate his poetic so much as embody it. Additionally, the issues raised by this introduction include those of autobiography and personality in post-modern writing, issues which came to dominate the residency, and these issues were raised, typically, not by confrontation but by constant reference to them in a de facto manner.

The following comments took about ten minutes for Berrigan to deliver. The remarks were an extemporaneous greeting and introduction, included here as a reference tool.

> . . . at 80 Langton Street I stand in the dock in judgment, condemned, and also to become informed, as my illustrious friends Anselm Hollo, Lorenzo Thomas and Kathy Acker before me have. I wish that I could be more controversial so that I could arouse massive discussion and seething ferment and fistfights. But I'm just a national treasure, like Anselm, except that Anselm is my older brother, by about three months. I'm going to read my book *The Sonnets* tonight, and tomorrow night I'm going to talk and I'm not going to lecture, I'm going to talk, and I hope that everyone here will, or some that are here will, talk as well. The title that is in the ads is accurate insofar as that goes but I am going to talk a lot about my work and what I think I did and what I thought I was doing when I was doing some of it at least, and what

I think I'm doing now. I'm going to talk in the Jesuit manner, with an injection of the Dominican hauture, but it will all be covered with Irish bullshit. Then on Friday a panel of experts will convene for your pleasure and entertainment. I've been assured by some of the members of that panel that all of the members of the panel will be very stimulating and exciting.

On Saturday, I'll be reading new works from the last two or three months. I have a new reading style, a new writing style, which I'll unveil here, it's my sort of spinster-aunt version of Anne Waldman's style. It's terrific, you'll love it completely I'm sure, everyone has. I'm going to read this book *The Sonnets*. I'll read it all the way through. I wrote it in 1963, roughly between March and July. I finished all but the last one, one, two or three days before my son David was born, my first child. Then after he was born, I was waiting for him to be released from the hospital, where he was born but they didn't want to let him out. He was, he seemed to be Chinese. Then I wrote the last one, I suddenly realized what the last one would be. It took me three months or whatever to write these. I wrote them, well I discovered them, I made the first one, or the first six, one night and then I couldn't quite believe my eyes. I was so excited I couldn't trust them [the poems], I put them in a drawer. Then about a week later I was looking at them again and I made six more. And then after that I did one or two more every day just about. I must have had some days off because it took me three months, but I wrote eighty-eight of them all together and there must be sixty some in here. It was very exciting when I was doing it and I didn't do anything else but these when I was doing them. In 1964 this book, not bound like this but with this cover, was published by "C" Press, which is my magazine. Ron Padgett did the work on it, but in 1967 it was picked up by Donald Allen at Grove Press and published by Grove. So it was my big success, in fact it was the book that . . . this mimeo edition we then mailed to every poet and anyone else that I would really like to have read it, by virtue of knowing their works that is. There was a lot of response, it was very nice — not always response directly to me but I would read with avid interest an interview with Creeley and lo and behold he would be announcing that there was this very interesting poet — me! I had to agree with him, but, you know . . . I came to New York in 1961 after graduate school and college at the University of Tulsa, and then I took seven months to do this M.A. thesis I was doing. Then I was living with Joe Brainard and we were going around seeing mostly pictures and then I moved into a place by myself and after several months and then that was the middle of '61 and within two years I had written this book. When I came to New York I hadn't written anything good at all. I came to New York to become this wonderful poet, to become a poet and I was to be very serious. Not to become but to be. To find out how to work at it. That only took about a year and a half, then I wrote this major work and there I was. Just as I thought I would be, in my inane stupidity. It's great. I wish something like that would happen again. For about ten years or more, twelve years, good friends of mine would go around saying "What

10. Cover by Joe Brainard for the original "C" Press edition of *The Sonnets*, 1964.

has Ted done since *The Sonnets?*" But writing this was the finish of something, not the beginning. When I wrote these, to set the record straight because I don't know that I've ever had occasion to speak this particularly, I didn't know any other poets at all. I hadn't met any other poets yet except I had met Kenneth Koch very briefly because he was a teacher of Ron's. I knew Ron Padgett and Dick Gallup, who were both writing poetry, and Joe Brainard who was a real artist, and is. Ron, Dick and Joe were all about nineteen. The only people I knew in New York were Ron's friends at college and a few landlords and some of the people mentioned in here. I wrote this entirely out of . . . . I hadn't been to very many poetry readings, had never given one, I guess I hadn't done anything. I was just this bumpkin with a Master's degree—I was old enough to have done something so I had done something, but I didn't write it out of being this person that I am here. It was by writing it that I became the someone who is the someone a good many years younger who is here. Writing it I was, I don't know how I had the nerve. Still it was not out of a literary scene, in terms of social literary scene, but it was very much out of a literary scene, in terms of my own head. I did write this as total discovery, I wasn't just discovering the sonnet, I had spent two or three years paying attention to the sonnet, partly because it seemed a congenial place for me and also partly because somebody had said that you couldn't do this, and it's my nature, as it is many people's, to then do that. I had never heard of the word "modernism," so I wasn't trying to be modern, or any other ism, in that way. I was trying to be new, in some sense. I was conscious that I was being new but I had spent a lot of time before writing, attempting to do various things that seemed to be new. The right way to do things because it was new. For me at that point the people like Creeley and O'Hara and Olson already were traditions, certainly by '63. I had been reading their poems since '56, '57, since Ron was in touch with those people from Tulsa, by virtue of the [White Dove] Review. I had learned already I think that what was as far as formal breakthroughs went, I didn't see much of any of that in The New American Poetry. Not too much anyway, some maybe but what was new, really new, of my own time in The New American Poetry seemed to me to be more a matter of a stance toward writing, toward reality in the way it could put down not a matter of formal means, the formal means, certainly from a literary Robert Creeley of that time even to Phil Whalen, seemed to me to be an extension of tradition. Although Phil I did think was not involved in literary formal breakthroughs, he was already through, it was just on the other hand he was this hick from the upper Northwest, and he had it all going for him. But I couldn't understand. I wanted to be like Big Bob Creeley and write Arthurian . . . . So this is a Horatio Alger story . . .

Berrigan's technique is inclusive of his complete life circumstances. In the ten-minute introduction, he manages to incorporate the names of Anselm Hollo, Lorenzo Thomas, Kathy Acker, Anne Waldman, an anecdote about the birth of his son David, Ron Padgett several times, Donald Allen, Joe Brainard,

Dick Gallup, Frank O'Hara, Charles Olson and Kenneth Koch. This is not to imply that this was wholly inappropriate: these were the initial remarks of a major public appearance, and history was very much on Berrigan's mind. Rather it was part of the ongoing incorporation of those close or once close to Berrigan into both his work and his personal mythology building. Moreover, an audience is free to react in a range from admiration and acceptance to shock and distrust. What is really occurring however is that the audience is being coerced into dealing with the theatrical nature of any such public self-presentation. While ultimately valuable, the question is whether this is in any way Berrigan's intention. Are the outrageous lines, calculated confessions, sincere introspection, planned confrontations, and self-described "Irish bullshit" a strategy to have us question the role of hero? As Ron Silliman put it in *Soup* magazine, is it all "ego, shapeless and banal, or is there an underlying commitment to achieving a unity?"

Since one sits on the bench in judgment or stands at the dock to be judged, Berrigan's opening sentence indicates a certain confusion about the intention of the San Francisco community in its invitation to come to 80 Langton. Whatever subplots might be taking place among specific personalities, to allow such dramas to characterize an entire residence in confrontational terms is demeaning to both artist and audience. Berrigan's later, generous willingness to struggle with his awkward public estimation of his contribution to American poetry was therefore unnecessary. It proceeded from a basic misapprehension of the power and responsibility of the rostrum. Remarks about a desire to be "controversial" and "entertaining" are similarly inappropriate, if well-disposed. Alternately, his apparently sincere offer to "become informed" was a point of juncture with the audience, containing so many of his peers, former students, acquaintances and readers. These people were in attendance because they were anxious to define what exactly is of importance in contemporary American poetry. Perhaps the choice of a historical, retrospective cast to the residence was a planning error.

The Sonnets continue to be a source of great poetic value, and the reading Berrigan gave of it was moving, inspiring and thought-provoking. His remarks about their conception contain the apparent contradiction that while they were the finish, not the start of something, he "didn't write it out of being this person that I am here. It was by writing it that I became the someone who is the someone who is here." Similarly, hindsight informs us that his circle of friends very quickly became central to the New York poetry scene. Therefore his feeling of having not known any poets at the time of writing *The Sonnets* is difficult for us to understand from this point in history, when the names of Gallup, Clark, Padgett, et al. are established. Yet Berrigan's recollection of the origins of the book do not strike me, on rereading, as disingenuous (as they did when heard live). Rather, a close reading reveals that this is not an assertion on Berrigan's part that *The Sonnets* descended upon his innocent consciousness while he sat meditating in Tompkins Square Park one day. Berrigan is simply maintaining that while he was still an outsider to any established literary scene, he was quite aware of what was happening in the poetry scene in the U.S. in terms of new writing, and had thought and studied quite a bit about it. Ironically, his feelings that Creeley, O'Hara and Olson were traditions from which he felt a need to distinguish himself formally, can be a way of looking at Berrigan's own position as perceived by many younger poets in San Francisco. Certainly, however, the gesture of inviting Berrigan to 80 Langton Street was made out of respect and interest in the work, all the work. Whatever the ultimate origin and sources that Berrigan drew upon in constructing *The Sonnets,* the fact remains that they are probably our most valuable document summing up literary events of that era, and that in many ways they achieved a vital breakthrough in American poetry.

The Sonnets are a series of "machines," selections from found materials organized by the mechanics of Berrigan's inspiration. He mentioned during the reading that, for instance, "From a Secret Journal" was based on a manuscript that Joe Brainard had given him, even though in the end very little of Brainard's work made it into the text. Other sources mentioned included unfinished works by Padgett and Berrigan himself.

Because the subject matter is the stretching of language's ability to make meaning, *The Sonnets* retain a contemporary sound, if somewhat lyrical and at times slightly weighted down by uninspired imagery ("my dream a crumpled horn / in advance of the broken arm"). There are exceptions to the technique of displacement and leaps in texture and syntax, in a more O'Hara-like "I did this, I did that" style. Also, there is the signature use of such names as Richard Gallup's, not as a personal reference but as a found object useful for its Western connotation in the final shootout of that poem, "Poem in the Traditional Manner."

Further levels of complexity are added with poems that repeat in rearranged, cut-up form, whole sections of other poems in the book, thus giving the work a self-referential, echoing sound. Like the composer Alvin Lucier taping the repetition of one paragraph over and over in a room until the listener gets a sense of the effects of the architecture of that room on sound, Berrigan interweaves the syllables in use to permanently capture a psychological space and time.

There are also some fairly straightforward narrative poems in the third person. Berrigan's live reading reinforced the impression that there are certain sonnets which are definitive, and others which are included for pacing, variety and content. These are read with an earnestness and clearly intentioned voice that forms an identity between the I and a deep commitment in the author's intellect and emotions which are unmistakable in their power. These, again, are for me the ones which are the least narrative and the ones not in the third person, but the more disjunct and "difficult."

One interesting sidelight was the appearance in the reading of poems not published in the Grove Press edition, edited out, for various reasons. Many lines from these poems are reused in published poems.

A theme often employed in the series is that of stopping and starting: some poems literally start over several times and "Sonnet XL," which ends "I recall / My Aunt Annie and begin," is exactly at the halfway point. A major theme of gunfire in the old Western context is raised, as it was in the Gallup reference, and elsewhere. Berrigan explains that his dream is "gunfire inside my poems," an idea further explored years later in *Clear the Range*.

There is a certain retreat from the more severe cut-up method of the first third of the book in the second third, more of an anecdotal feel, as though Berrigan were shoving that whole section into the same drawer into which he had shoved the first six poems after writing them. Then the fragmentation comes back for the balance of the book. The difference now is that the language of radical juxtaposition of phrases of the first third of the book is in these last, quite wonderful poems, combined with a more personal narrative thrust. The quotation process accelerates until whole poems are made up of parts of other poems, and the last technique introduced is the use of images from preceding lines of preceding poems so that the poems are quite literally connected.

—Renny Pritikin

BRING
ON
THE
FLIES
!

11. Ted Berrigan, self-portrait. Collection of Ron Padgett.

The Chicago Report: A Note

RON PADGETT

Ted Berrigan was a natural mimic and parodist, blending voices and vocabularies with Joycean astuteness and Rabelaisian glee. At certain points in this letter, he parodies a voice common to Tulsa, Oklahoma, where we first met. In some ways, this letter is a take-off on Kerouac. Ted felt free to make fun of any writer, sacred cow, or cause, even causes he believed in, such as civil rights. He loved to say big, outrageous, funny things, and although some readers might find this letter more tasteless than amusing — the risk run by certain kinds of humor — I hope no one will make the mistake of interpreting it literally.

The Chicago Report

TED BERRIGAN

Dear Ron:

Here's a stab at the Chicago Report.

Friday Morning, November 15th.
Happy Birthday to me. Kate gives me some orange socks and David gives me a big hammer. *Mediterranean Cities* from you arrives in the mail. Birthday greetings from Anne and Lewis and George and Iris and plenty of others. Last night in The Mill, a bar, Art Rosenbaum, author of a book, *The Banjo,* sang Happy Birthday to me, and Esther, a terrific thin girl, gave me a birthday card that said FUCK YOU, and inside, may I? I didn't. So, I feel great! Eat. Smoke Dope. Pack extra underwear, razor, Frank O'Hara, newspapers and pot into tuxedo-carrying bag. Ready.

Henry arrives, 12:00 P.M. in red 1959 Volkswagen, we go. Bye-bye Sandy, bye-bye kids, bye-bye Iowa City.

On the road. We drive twenty miles. Henry grins. We listen to corny radio songs like "When I Was a Blackbird" I mean "If." Henry smokes Marlboros, I smoke Chesterfields. We discuss Henry's poetry. I say, it's out to lunch, but it's good. Henry hands me a piece of paper. I open and read it, and grin:

Hi Ted!
Here is a poem for you
on your birthday
Aren't you reading it
speeding across Iowa in my Volkswagen
your great naked smile on your face?
When I learned that today was to be your
birthday, I said, I must buy Ted a present for
his birthday, but when it came around, I didn't
have any money left. Poems are better birthday
presents if they are from famous poets, like yours
to Anne. I send you with this one, however
a warm glow from me to you, issuing from my
affection for you, like a cup of coffee in the
morning which never ceases to bring delight, and get
the day started off right.
We should do our best to see that
you have a marvelous and poetic birthday weekend
in Chicago, seeing Kenneth and all the friends.
If you are having a bad time, just tell me
and I will give you a balloon and stick of peppermint.
                                              —Henry

So, a warm glow fills up the car, which is also filled up with Henry's complete works, DADA by Motherwell, oil, clothes and us. We go on happily through Iowa, flat but really rolling countryside, green and brown beneath blue sky, for one more foot. Then Henry's vw breaks. Ack! Henry flips out, but I am glowing and think it is wonderfully funny, like in this report.

We stop in a few country gas stations, where no one knows shit, but everyone is friendly. Then we drive twenty miles an hour for an hour, and get to Davenport, thirty-five miles from Iowa City. It is now almost 4:00. We leave the vw at a vw fixers, and the fixer gives us a ride to the bus station. The bus leaves in one minute! Henry buys *Playboy* and I buy *The New Yorker*, and we get on the bus.

We sit and read. *The NY* is boring and takes thirty minutes to read. The jokes are ok. *Playboy* is boring, too. The girls are fat and goitery-looking with titties too big, mouths too uninteresting, and faces like cocker spaniels. I sleep. Henry makes time with a girl across the aisle. We are starving. The bus stops in Hicksville, the 300th stop, for one minute, and I tell Henry to get the candy bars. He returns chagrined. The bus driver said nobody gets off. I say, wait here.

I go to the front of the bus, the door is shut. I press a few forbidden buttons, the door opens. I saunter off like Broderick Crawford, and the driver outside avoids my eyes. I buy fifty candy bars. I get back on. Henry eats a few candy bars, I do too, and we give the rest to a few girls.

Henry is burdened with about ten complete changes of wardrobe plus tuxedo and fifty books for our two-day stay in Chicago.

We get to Chicago, after a few great behind-the-eyeball dreams while almost asleep in the twilight and early evening unreal bus light. It is now 8:00 P.M.

Off the bus, into the bus station, tired, sleepy, dirty, bus-ragged. Call up Paul Carroll, to sleep free in his mansion. I do. He says, hi buddy and all that blab no stay here. George Starbuck stay here but you come dinner Sunday night and we talk plenty. I say, you great guy Paul mighty good to talk to you. Ha ha. Is Kenneth here. Yes. He's at giant millionaire's party no bums allowed at the home of Mr. Arkadin (Antonow). I say, sure, good-bye.

I tell Henry we can't stay at Paul Carroll's, but we can go to the great millionaire party leave it to me.

Eat. We eat hamburgers served by luscious young Negress. Good. Then we go to find a hotel. Out in dirty Chicago. All downtown Chi is like Times Square only grosser. I stop a big ugly cop. Where? He says, "there." There is the Hotel Sherman. Big Capitalistic Hilton. In we go. Twenty dollars one room one night. Ok. No? Out we go. Take cab to the Holiday Inn Motel. Miles. How much? Twenty-two dollars. Fuckin' Shit. Back out, walk.

Into a few nigger hotels. Rooms? No sah. Ugh! Into middle-class white hotel. Any rooms? Haughty middle-aged tired lady prick says, huh, are you kidding. No commie dope beatnik hippie shit flingers here. Oh yeah, I forgot.

So, back to the downtown Hotel Sherman. No rooms left. Henry gets an idea. He calls up the Lafayette, almost as ritzy as the Sherman. Reservations, yes sir, how many, two, fine, sir, come right over. Ha ha. We do. They shit their pants, look us over plenty, but let us in. Up we go. Eleventh floor, twenty-one dollars, what the fuck!

Into room, turn on TV, watch *Star Trek* getting over. The Captain is dead, and Mr. Spock and Bones are pissed off at each other. Smoke joints. Take pills. Call up Mr. Arkadin.

Hello? This is Ted Berrigan, is Kenneth Koch there? Just give me your number and he'll call you back. Ok (shit). Hang up.

The Captain is not really dead. He was trailing along in the jet stream behind the ship. Ding-a-ling. Hello. Hello, this is Kenneth Koch. Kenneth! What's happening. Kenneth says: Ted! Happy Birthday!

Bong! Another warm glow. K says, want to come over? We say, you better believe it. He says, I'll ask Henry Rago. Henry Rago says, "groovy." OK, see you in one minute.

Hang up, put on really great tuxedos, with suspenders, bow ties, cummerbund, and hippie beads made for me by Iris. Henry does same. Out we go, down elevator, sneer at desk clerks and other jackoffs, and away.

Ack! Where the fuck is the place? Doorman never heard of it (Carlisle Apts). Look in phone book. Not there. Holy shit. Walk around, can't find it. Eureka. Call up Paul Carroll (incidentally sick in bed with flu). Where the fuck is it? He tells me. We go. Taxi. Whoosh. Carlisle Apts, overlooking beautiful Lake Michigan. Rooftop Room. Up we go, into room.

Wow! Billions of little drinkies! Get some. Maybe two hundred people (all whiteys except waiters). Women in $500 dresses with little titties hanging out. Men all have same kinds of suits on, just like us. Young rock group blasting away at Mach 28. Great.

Where's Kenneth? (It's now 11:30.) He is dancing with lush blonde who has taken off his coat and is tweaking his suspenders. Now she has her whole arm through one of his suspenders. K is grinning broadly and executing some kind of ritzy penguin hops. The music stops. We attack Kenneth. He says, Com'stai! Andiamo! Sacre bleu! Pastafazol! etc, and throws his arms around me. I say, "Where's the pussy?"

Kenneth laughs. I say, this is Henry Pritchett, a poet from Texas. Kenneth grins. His hair is three feet long but combed beautifully (K's, not H's). Kenneth and Henry love each other.

Kenneth says this is a crazy party, excuse me. He grabs luscious blonde and hops onto dance floor. Henry and I drink. Beautiful waitress goes by. I pat her on thigh and say, dinner? She says, maybe. Goes into kitchen, and returns with absolutely beautiful food. Two kinds of meat, turkey and roast beef. Broccoli wrapped in pancakes, other delicacies all over the plate. Henry & I eat in one second. Wonderful. I light a Chesterfield and he lights a Marlboro.

Henry's eyes are popping out at a woman with a black and white no front dress, with big sleek juicy titties hanging brazenly under her nose. Go. He goes, gets her, and they dance. People stop in wonderment at Henry's Texas-style dancing, energetic, galloping, beautiful. Kenneth dances over, laughing. I watch. A little guy who looks like Wally Cox comes over to me. I think maybe he likes me. He leans close to me and says, "Fuck Communism!"

Holy shit, a fan! He's a nice guy, name of Ralph Mills, from Ill. U. He says, you read here next year, two hun fifty? I say, terrific. At that moment a vision of loveliness in a white neck high tight demure rich and movie-star (Jeanne Crain) dress comes over to me and says, dance? So we do.

I rub my leg against her pussy a little, and squeeze her just a little to see if she responds. She does. She then says, as the dance ends, come and meet my husband.

Her husband is good looking in a stupid drunk way, like Robt Wagner w/o viciousness (actually, like RW as cocker spaniel). He says, I'm in advertising. It's a visual medium and so Poetry is not my line. I say, very interesting, excuse me, drinkie. I go, have twenty drinkies. Henry dances incredibly with every good-looking woman. I talk to Kenneth and Ralph Mills. I meet Daryl Hine. Hooray, a real live person, very sharp. He says, I like *Bean Spasms.* I say, we send you more *Bean Spasms* for *Poetry.* He says, maybe. Ha ha, I was just kidding, Dwight, I mean Daryl. But actually, he is interesting and I like him. He says, tell me about some poets. I say, ok, who. He says, Clayton Eshleman. I say, total loser. He breathes sigh of relief, and says, I met him last week. Henry gave him a prize. Then he says, Jim Carroll. I say, totally great. He says, I just took a long poem of his, and could actually have taken all he sent me. Then he says Charles Goldman. I say pretty interesting, could be terrific sometime, I like him. He says, me too.

Ok. I meet Henry Rago. He is a worried little man, looks like a Jewish version of HHH, tho not such a prick. All other people at party are rich pricks, trustees and socialites.

Party begins to get done. I chat with Mr. Arkadin. He looks like Aristotle Onassis's younger wastrel brother, and has a special tux that looks like a yacht captain's evening coat. I say pretty nice coat you got there jack, you look like a yacht captain. Ha ha. He says, thank you, it is nice isn't it. Then he says, come downstairs to my apartment for drinkies in a minute with Mr. Koch and Mr. Rago (and, I add in my head, Mr. Pritchett). Sure, I say, envisioning the bare-breasted girls in a more intimate setting. I tell Henry, he says, great. We chat with Henry Rago, whom I introduce to Henry Pritchett. Henry says, what do you do? Ha ha, I roar with laughter. Then Kenneth comes up, very red-faced.

He says, Henry [Rago] I'm leaving. I'm not coming to your dinner, and I'm not sure I'm reading either. He is steaming. Henry Rago says Holy Shit! No, he doesn't say that, he says, what's the matter Kenneth, in a soothing but worried tone. Kenneth says, Mr. Arkadin just came up to me and said, ok Kock, or Crotch, or whatever your name is, lets go downstairs for a drink. Henry Rago says, he was just kidding you Kenneth. Kenneth says, I don't have to take any shit from these assholes, Henry. (Kenneth also says I don't give a shit for you *or* your magazine.) I told him to go fuck himself. Henry Rago faints. No, only figuratively. Kenneth says, is he coming to the dinner tomorrow. HR says, he's on the board, Kenneth. Kenneth says, then I'm not. In fact, I'm going to go back and hit him. Kenneth goes. Mr. Arkadin has split wisely. Kenneth comes back. I say, lets go find him and kick his ass, Kenneth. Henry says yeah! What's happening. Henry (Rago) says, Holy Shit!

So, me and Henry and Kenneth split. Kenneth cools down. He asks the bandleader where it's at. The bandleader tells him and the three of us go off to find it.

Henry and Kenneth rap every minute. We wander thru Chi's swinging places in our tuxes. We go in little bars full of students and girls and music and drink beers. We go in hundreds of lame places. Kenneth and Henry try to pick up quim. Everybody laughs. Then we go in bookstore and admire *Poetry* with Jimmy Schuyler's name on it. Kenneth buys a detective story and I buy the EVO[*East Village Other*]. We talk to some spades and they say, where's the dope? Henry P. says, we have no dope, but this here is K. Koch, the famous poet, who gets $500 for a reading. Kenneth beams with pride, speechless, but laughing, while the spades say holy shit. Then we all go to eat—me, K, H and the spades. We eat cheeseburgers and ffs and drink rootbeers, and then split. first we borrow twenty dollars from Kenneth. He says, Henry makes me feel very happy every time I see him. Henry says, Kenneth is wonderful. I say, holy shit. We go back to the hotel, smoke the joints, sleep.

SECOND DAY

We wake up, 2:30 P.M. Check out time, 3:00, ugh. Henry calls up room service and says, send coffee. I turn on TV. Michigan is playing Wisconsin. Ron Johnson scores five touchdowns and breaks the rushing record of 468 yards in one game, set only last week by Eddy Podolak, the Iowa quarterback turned tailback. I ponder whether or not this pisses me off, but it doesn't.

Me and Henry have a conference, over coffee and a few joints. We don't have much money. But Henry has a few oil company credit cards. So, we call up a travel agency and ask them what hotels or motels honor oil company credit cards. We find out that some do.

So. Packing up, getting ready to go, out we go, fuck off horrible Hotel Lafayette, fuck off Times Square of Chicago. Chicago is a real "big city" but other than that it's horrible. (Henry loves it and I guess I would too if.)

Taxi to a big motel overlooking Lake Michigan on Lake Shore Drive, just down the street from Kenneth, and just down the street from the Petroleum Building where the reading is being held, and just UP the street from the RR station.

Into motel, motel clerks are very nice. We are on the fifth floor. Big airy room, lots of light, full wall-length glass doors lead out to swimming pool. Temp. is 45 and it is raining slightly. We unpack. Turn on TV. Michigan 50 - Wisconsin 14. It is now 4:30. Smoke a few joints, down we go to have a Bloody Mary. The cocktail party, dinner and then reading begins at 5:30, but first, a few chores.

Write postcards to you and everybody else. Go out, mail them, take cab to the public library, where Henry xeroxes a few poems to give Kenneth. Rush through the rain to the ladies lingerie store, to buy bikini panties for Patty's birthday. Rush to the Chicago Art Museum to see the Dada, Surrealism and horseshit show. Taxi back to the motel.

Now. Smoke a few joints, listen to the ball scores. Iowa is playing mighty Ohio State. Shit. They lost. But wait, the score was only 33-28. Iowa is terrific. Last year they were 1-9, and only four seniors on the first two strings. So, put on tuxes, pause wistfully, me, for a last twinge of disappointment, and then rush out the door into the taxi and up to the Petroleum Building.

At the door to it, we meet Paul Carroll. Hi folks, and his wife, who loves Henry and vice versa. Henry puts his arm around her. We go upstairs. Inside, millions of drinkies, talk to Marvin Bell — the boy midget, George Starbuck — the hometown George Plimpton, don't know nobody else.

What a finky crowd. Two hundred for dinner. Eight at a table. At the table with me and "Mrs. Ted Berrigan" (who was Henry), six jackoffs. They begin an incredible conversation about whether or not most young people are really into anything, or are they just jackoffs. It's the table vs. Henry. I eat. Henry baffles everybody by being Henry and they don't know what to do. They are all a little tired, except for Henry, and not that interested in their own voices. Henry however is tremendously earnest, and also tremendously interested in what he has to say. He wipes them out. I have retreated into some back room of my head, and am getting ready for the reading.

For dinner we have lousy food, but two table wines.

Then, at 8:00, we go upstairs, or maybe it was downstairs, for the reading. Two hundred jackoffs in tuxedos, meet another couple of hundred people in street dress. We do. Kenneth goes backstage, where Anne Sexton is priming her pump with hysteria, and I go to the men's room.

I come out, a solitary figure in tuxedoed splendor, to be met by a radiant Iris.

(Ha ha, it was all planned, but almost misfired due to slow mail, etc. etc.)

We are very happy to see each other. We go sit down with Henry. The reading begins. Kenneth is introduced by Henry Rago, who says that K is the most influential and one of the best poets in USA. Kenneth comes out, plays a few riffs on the can-you-hear-me-in-the-back theme, as is his habit, and then knocks everybody out for about an hour with a really great reading. He reads "Sleeping w/Women," "The Pleasures of Peace" and a few oldies but goldies, as well as a new work, "Faces," which was so inspiring I can't even remember a single line. Iris and I are hugging each other and grinning. Henry is dumbfounded by the arrival of Iris, and my obvious lack of surprise, and also dazzled by Kenneth. Applause.

Then Anne Sexton is introduced by Daryl Hine. She makes a dramatic entrance in a white and black topless gown, very long, looking like Anne Bancroft, though insane. She has a kind of fresh-from-the-snake-pit look. Her poems are shit. She stinks.

Then its over, and we all split to a party at some spoiled society bitch's house. This here chick is totally luscious. Kenneth pats her on the pussy a few times. We have a lot of drinks, and talk to Jim Tate and Marvin Bell and Kenneth and Henry, but mostly I talk to Iris.

Iris and I split and go back to the motel. The rest go to some party. In the motel the beds are right next to each other. We get there at 2:00. Henry comes at 5:00. We all sleep til 7:00. Iris and I go out for breakfast at a spade breakfast joint. She has to catch a train at 8:00. I take her to the train. Good-bye. It was really lovely. And it really was. I buy the *Sunday Trib*, walk back to the room, read it, smoke a few joints, go to sleep.

THIRD DAY

Sunday afternoon. I wake up at 3:00. Tired, but feeling good. Smoke some Chesterfields, turn on the TV. Detroit is playing Baltimore.

The hotel restaurant is too expensive. So, we pack our things, smoke the last of the pot, and check out.

Taxi to the bus station, and put our things in a big locker.

Digging the streets. Dig the Picasso sculpture. Dig Wimpy's, where we dig the cheeseburgers. Henry says, "They have Wimpy's in Paris and London, too. I saw them." Then we dig the streets some more, dig the people, and dig the postcard scene.

Then, into another taxi, and off to Paul Carroll's. We debate whether or not to take the acid now. Before dinner, or after dinner? After. Ok.

At Paul's, Henry kisses the hostess, and we have a delicious dinner, with fellow guests Jim Tate, the Yale Younger Poet for 1967, and Dennis Schmitz, the Big Table Prize Poet for 1969. Dennis Schmitz has the flu and can't eat. Paul Carroll is warm and friendly in his inimitable manner, and I kind of have a good time. His apartment is nice, roomy, lots of paintings and photos and books and green plants and light. His wife is terrific, I finally decide.

Jim Tate I like, but could easily not.

So, dinner gets finished, and it's off to the University of Chicago, to hear the two poets of dinner read. Henry and I secretly decide to take the acid. We do.

Paul introduces the poets. They read. Tate isn't bad, but not that good. He's wild ok, but wild academic, which is only mildly interesting. Dennis Schmitz is ok, but his poetry is boring. We wait for the acid to hit us, and eye the girls. I think of Tony Walters. There is only one beautiful girl, a soft blonde girl with a purple dress.

The reading gets over, we start for a party. We will have to leave soon, to catch a 12:30 bus to Iowa City.

The acid hits. Totally freaked out but maintaining a calm exterior, I enter the little apartment where the party is. Woolworth's furniture, no interesting paintings, everybody shy, not too many people, wine. I have some wine and bread, sit in a chair, a big easy chair, smoke a Chesterfield.

Henry heads straight for the beautiful girl. I lose track of him. I am suspended between an acid trip and a party. I drop the burning end of my cigarette into the depths of the chair. I try to put it out. I think I succeed, but just in case, I move over to the couch. Hundreds of hours pass. Henry has disappeared. I drink some wine, most of the people have gone into other rooms. A young kinky blonde girl about seventeen comes and talks to me. I mention Korea, and she says, "I wasn't even born then." I say, terrific.

I notice people are carrying cups of water over and pouring them into the chair. Very interesting. It seems to be smoldering. I hear someone say ". . . don't know how it happened." I forget it.

Paul Carroll comes over and says, ride downtown? I say, what time? He says, 11:45. I say, ok. Then I say to Jim Tate: Tell Henry, Bus. He says ok.

We go. The ride downtown is sensational, I take millions of rich warm side trips. After years we get to the bus station and have the Irish good-bye scene. I can hardly keep from bursting out laughing.

Then, into the bus station. Inside, it's horrible. I shudder, and begin to feel a little sick, a little lost, a little scared, a little crazy.

In my back pocket are postcards. I think: mail. It takes me hours to get stamps, but I do, lick them and then go outside and mail the cards. Then I know I am a great competent guy, just a soldier on leave in a strange city like lots of other times and nothing to fear. But Chicago faces are ugly.

I cross the street outside the bus station in the rain, and go to contemplate the Picasso sculpture. By now I am tired (tho I wasn't then) so I will not go into the incredible things I had happen in my art brain there. Then, back to the bus station, Henry arrives, zonked, but happy to see me. We buy tickets, and have fifteen cents left. Get bags, get on bus.

Long interesting mild and thoughtful bus trip to Iowa City, to arrive at 6:00 A.M. Monday morning, disturbed only once pleasantly when Henry got off bus and bought us M & M's.

Iowa City. I get off, shake hands with Henry, say, see you later, I'm going home. He grins and says, see you, I'm going into the bus station and this beautiful girl I met on the bus here is going to buy me coffee.

> See you.
> Love,
> Ted
> November 30, 1968

12. "Personal Nancy Love" — Cartoon by Joe Brainard and Ted Berrigan.

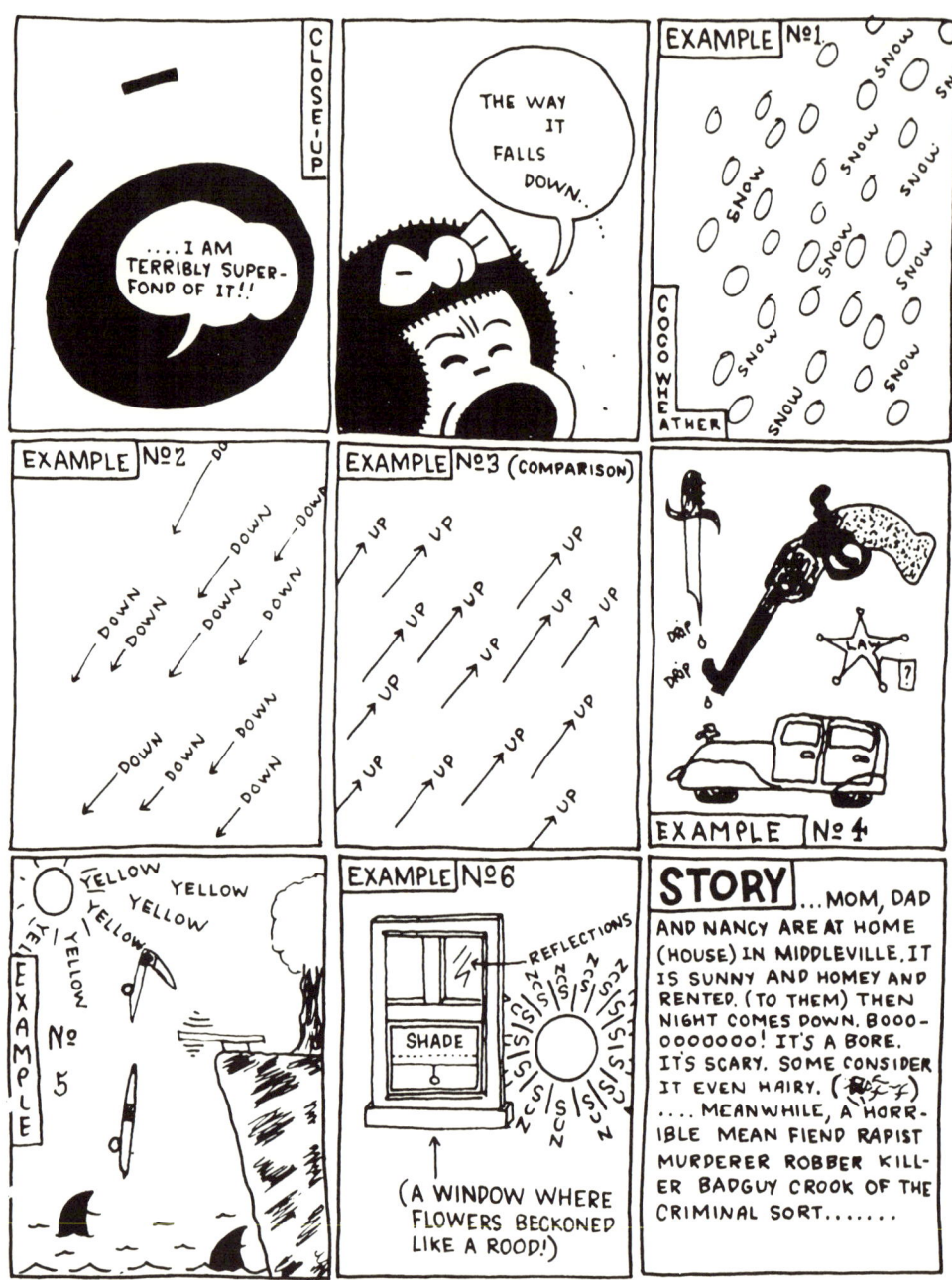

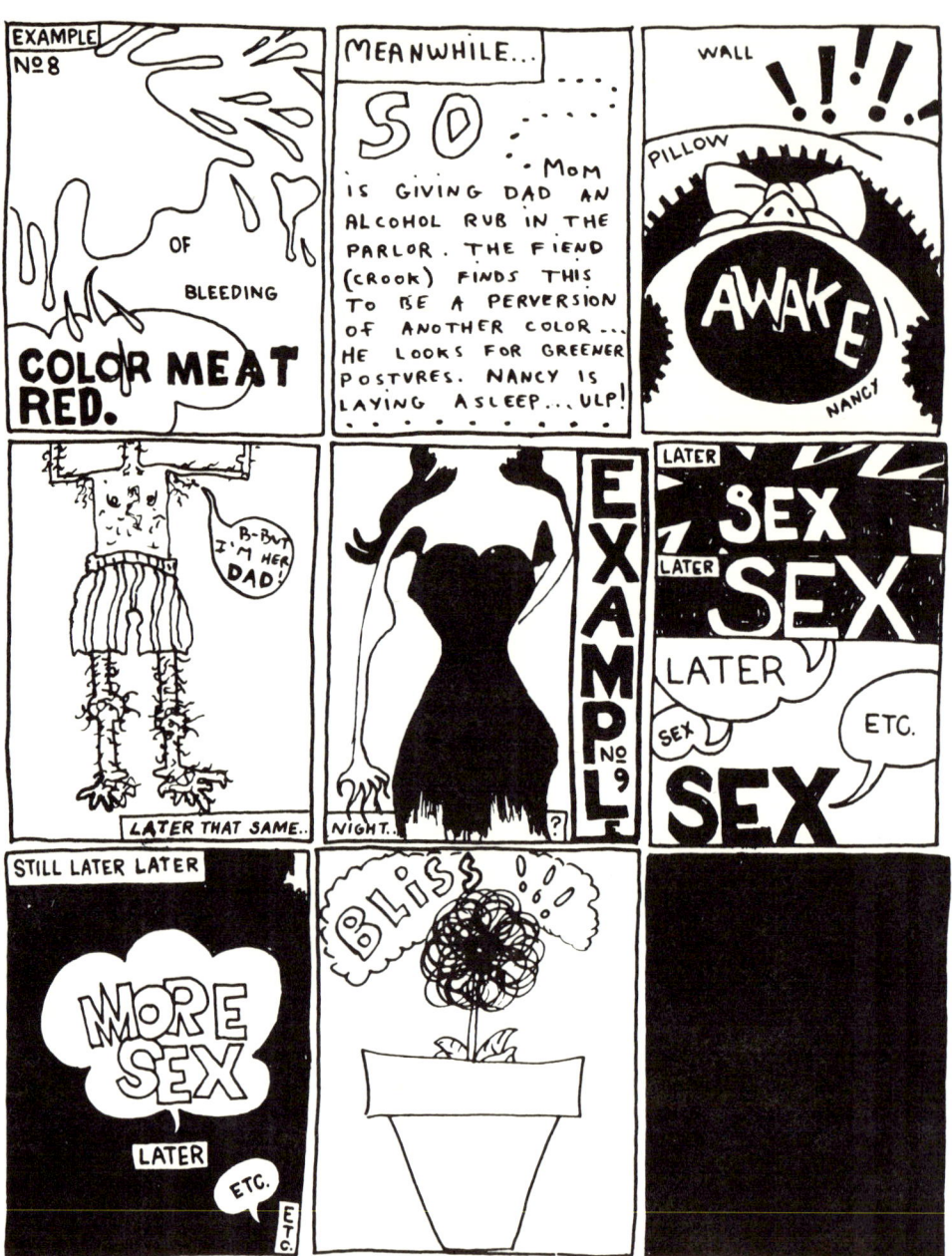

Letter to Joe Brainard

TED BERRIGAN

Dear Joe

Nice to get a letter from you, always a great pick-up for me. I'm "happy" here, and writing a lot, maybe twenty new poems. I never make copies, but watch for four in the new *World* and two in some new *Paris Review.* I'm happy for you about your new place. *Many Happy Returns* sold out, I guess you know, and is begin reprinted now. Allen Ginsberg was here last week and gave a super reading of *Howl* plus new poems. I cried yesterday, because Jack Kerouac died. It's nice to be alone, tho lonely a lot. I keep busy. I feel as if another "new life" has been going on for me since the middle of last year, and tho I feel older than in New York, I don't feel "old" any more, I feel alive and heading for "more" and "bigger and better" Ted Berrigan Works, of which some "small and new" works are arriving bi-weekly. I'm holding them in the drawers, and praying over them (their future bigger ones). I see better. At least I think I do. And mellower. I read lots of I Remember at Larry's [Larry Fagin's] and it's SO beautiful! You are the best writer I have ever read and no one else ever could write your works. I love you plenty, tho I never say so, and tho we do have long and difficult silences sometimes, I never worry about us. I hope you don't, either. Actually, I never think you do (worry about my love for you, that is). I saw a movie I liked plenty, *Alice's Restaurant.* I came in in the middle, and saw it to the end and then to the middle. I think that was a lucky break for me. I can't write about Frank, either, for about the same reasons you said. Frank is Frank. But I'll love to read what others write, and I like to hear stories about Frank. I haven't read any good poems about him. I wish Larry Rivers would write about him. I dig Larry's writings a lot. Ken should write about him. He's told me some terrific stories about Frank. I don't want to, but I love to talk about him, and do, all the time. I guess I think about him nearly every day. I'll write about him someday. Actually, I'd rather have Frank write about me.

Are you still doing another "C" Comics? I'd like to do something, but I don't know what. You could use "Living With Chris," but maybe something new would be better. I'd like ours to be beautiful. I'll be in NYC in November, for my birthday, the 15th of November. We can get together and I can see what you are doing, and have done, with others, and show you my new poems, and maybe we can figure something out. Maybe something "about" all our friends, maybe something about Frank. Or Edwin. Something about Anne Waldman.

(I'm thinking I guess of a comic strip with people we like in it, plus Nancy and Archie and Tarzan and the Hulk. Or anyone else. Dostoevski. Larry Fagin. Joe LeSueur. de Kooning). How about an interview comic strip? Let's interview each other about sex, absolutely straight, what we like, who's attractive (boys and girls for both), etc. I'll talk about my experiences with boys, you with girls, and vice versa. Or is that too much do you think? Or maybe we could just do a writing work (conversation, written down, maybe even by mail, with the idea of it being true, straight, friendly, casual, chatty, factual, curious, and a "work" too?) Does any of that sound promising? It, since your work, and even before (What I like to do in bed) has been buzzing around in my head. There's so much to be talked there, so that you (that is, I) can hear what I might say (I mean, I don't know what I might say, but I'd love to hear myself talk about what I like to do in bed, what I do actually do in bed, how many different situations there are always changing . . . in other words, a real personal impersonal true life art natural work work). Is any of that clear? Do you think we could bring something like that off? Or even get started? The thing is, so few people talk about "that" ("it") like real (ordinary) people, which I think very much that I am and that you are, that it seems like a real idea. Write me if you have any ideas on that line. The pills, which should have reached you by now, or soon, by Airmail Special Delivery in a secret package with two boring books, are pretty good. I don't know their name, but they are 10 mg amphetamine. One is nice, two are hot stuff, and three, far out and millions of little dots on the page. I'm on two now, plus a valium, tranquilizer, so that I can go sleep in an hour or so. It's 6:00 A.M. now. Lewis knows you meant it about money, Joe. He felt like a million dollars that you felt to offer, and so has enough now. He's in Bolinas with Tom Clark, and doing fine. I talked with him last night. We did a work together while he was here, and had a warm and good time together. He's ok. He can handle it ok. He and Anne are both ok. And Michael is, too. Even if all that is going on. I guess it was due.

What painters do you like now? I don't see much painting here, and art itself is temporarily not so exciting, I guess, except for your work, and George's struggles, and Donna's. Next to de Kooning, I think you are the best, even if you aren't interested in putting yourself in that position (that is, running for future president) right now. Your "combines" (or whatever the critics will eventually call them), were better than Rauschenberg's, and better than any-one's. Are you going to throw it all out the window again soon, and start from scratch and mess, or keep working at details and openness for a longer while? I'm sure you don't know that answer, but I feel that you can do big masterpieces any time you want to (I think I can, sometimes, too), but wanting to sure is hard, isn't it? Actually, Andy is a guy I'm interested in plenty, still. And Alex. Masterpieces isn't what I mean, actually, but just big facts. For example, I think John Ashbery is better than ever, but somehow not as exciting. My favorite poet in the world now that Frank is dead is Edwin Denby, and next, I guess, Ron. I like Anne and Lewis MacAdams a lot. I always want to read Jimmy, and I always want to read Larry Fagin. Harris Schiff is a younger guy whose works I'm getting to like. I really admire Michael Brownstein's works, and Jim Carroll's but it's not the same thing. Kenneth goes on being Kenneth and his works are a pleasure. The younger guys interest me most, plus old masters like Eliot, Keats, Shakespeare, Chaucer, D. H. Lawrence (his poems), Whitman, Philip Whalen. In fact, I'm still "in love" with Poetry. But, odd as it is to say, I don't think I'm being directly influenced by poetry so much anymore, as by where I'm living, climate, feeling of place, blue sky, my body, my feelings, memory and dreams. Only Frank's poems still send me right to the typewriter or the notebook. But then my poems don't come out like Frank, but like me in a new place, being quicker and mellower at the same time, more sweep, more grace (with no less awkwardness), longer lines, plenty of rhymes, tho not end line rhymes, more Irishness, a mellower joy. No less energy tho, I think. I read lots of poems aloud with Alice, my Iowa City girlfriend visiting me here. Poems I used to like and now do again. Edwin's poems (tho I always liked them), and guys from the thirties. Something's happening involving a turn around and a return by a new guy. So much for that, anyway. I guess I want to write some Odes. I guess I want to write poems like de Kooning writes about painting, like Frank does about painting (in *Kulchur*) or about Poetry in his essay on *Dr. Zhivago,* etc.

Tell Ken I loved *Album.* It was him, beautifully, plenty risky, mad, and so much more "real" and "good" than lots of people are going to notice. Your things were pretty right for it, too.

I'd love to write some collaborations with you (Ken) if we can ever make a serious "business" appointment, for the working hours, confer on the subject matter, set up a few W.A.S.P. rules (to thicken the plot), and then write a whole series, over a period of time, about what we always write about (Everything)! Not like mine and Ron's, but like Montgomery Clift and James Dean. Or maybe like A. J. Liebling and S. N. Behrman. Or how about like Cole Porter and Bobby Dylan (whoops! I don't think I can get it up "to" Dylan yet). How about like Cole Porter and A. J. Liebling?

13. Sandy, Ted, David and Kate Berrigan, New York City, 1965.

Or maybe like Dashiell Hammett and Boris Karloff? Or better yet, John Lennon and Paul McCartney, if they were as good as we are.

This seems to be turned into a letter to M'sieur Elmslie, tho I hear he's in Vermont. But the preceding was an unpaid blurb and enthusiastic pitch for *Album.*

Joe, I guess I'll go eat a few Rice Krispies, read the paper, smoke a Chesterfield King, or twenty-two or so, and take the walk I love to take across a town as the sun comes up (and I go down).

If there are future pills to be had I'll let you know. I sent 120, to cover the fifty and ten you sent. There may be more, but it's up in the air right now. Meanwhile, I'm looking around.

I'm also sending something else (besides pills), so watch for it.

Love and so long, Ted
October 22, 1969
Ann Arbor

From a Letter to Phoebe MacAdams

TED BERRIGAN

Phoebe,

For Christmas, I love you (and all the rest of the time, too). This year I give these presents to you: 1. Everything I know: it goes like this: You don't have to do anything ever you don't want to do. And you can do anything you want to, anytime. Since those are the facts, you can do anything. Just want to be doing anything you find yourself doing. Or, stop. Nobody has authority of any kind over anyone else. You are your own and your only ultimate authority. 2. I give you these: for Christmas, for you, and for you and Ocean; so they're partly for Lewis, too. Alas for $, you'll have to go buy them yourself, this time. Next time, hopefully, I'll get that pleasure. But not this penniless year. Buy these and label them from me (anytime). For you and Ocean, a real old-time Mother Goose (and not the baboon Dr. Seuss). Go to some old bookstore; every baby boy in the world needs a Mommy to sing him the stories of the tribe. He needs to sing, he needs you to sing first, happily, and for joy, not to teach. Then he'll sing, too. Sing early, sing always. The songs of all our Grandmas, Daddies, us, not new versions (tho "Rudolph" is fine) but Hickory Dickory Dock, which grows up to be "Annabel Lee" and "Dark as a Dungeon Way Down in the Mine." Three Bears, Three Little Piggies, The Big Bad Wolf, The Gingerbread House. Not TV (tho it's ok) but first from you, with love, in play. Every every day. They never forget, your sons, that you did that. Sang them all they knew. And for now life and now time, go find all the books Ruth Krauss wrote if you have to hire detectives even. They are the ones that sing in the blood, and what songs they have in them, those songs are good.

Ted Berrigan
Christmas 1971

14. Ted Berrigan and Donna Dennis, Calais, Vermont, 1969. Photograph by Joe Brainard.

Excerpts from Journals

DONNA DENNIS

2/20/70

Riding on the bus on the way back down Fifth Avenue I had a great "flash" as Ted would say. That what I want to do in art is show how I feel. And that showing how I feel is a great heroic helpful thing to do. And then I thought—in order to show how I feel I choose materials and manner that will best show, express for me how I feel. Simple.

Feeling was building up very strong. Later I went to Kenward's to pick up *Best and Company* and had coffee and wine with Kenward and Joe who were just finishing dinner. We (I) talked of Flavin, earthworks (esp. Bob Morris's whose lithographs I had seen that day—works that were *sculpture in the land* and made all other earthworks look like silly, spooking "Man was here" works. Morris's were beautiful to look at).

Anyway, the conversation broke the tension that I had hoped would carry me into some decision about my art. *Doing* it.

Later, though I had thought he'd spend the night at Yale, Ted arrived and we talked of making art, the need to know art history (yes), the need to be realistic about who you are and what you can do—and Alex Katz who seems to be (right now at least) Ted's favorite artist.

Ted talked of making art that shows you how to live—that does not just show feelings. He says *The Sonnets* just show feelings and that they are therefore of not that much use to anyone. He mentioned moral strength a number of times, especially in reference to Alex Katz. He also said he thought that if one used images, one needed to look around all the time for *more* images to use.

2/21/70

I am definitely entertaining the idea of using paint and canvas again, whether à la Katz (nice and solid and painterly and traditional) or à la Alan Shields (unstretched, dyed and stitched shaped canvas)—both of whom look good to me. The main thing is to get back into the joy of working again in a way that provides me with the artist's dialogue with his materials at a pace fast enough to be thrilling. I want to learn a lot from my art. I want to put my feelings into my art in a more intense way. I want it all to happen faster. I want more joy, more fun, more stimulation. I think about Matisse a lot (the fact that I can get *into* his paintings more than any paintings ever). I think about maybe trying to translate my experience with Matisse into *my* nowaday experience.

I went last week to MOMA and looked at Matisse and remembered the excitement I used to feel when I was sure *this* was what I was aiming for — this was what it was going to be like to be an artist (colors, brushstrokes, drawing, changing lines).

Ted said something the other day about finding a lot for today in great works of the recent past — that you can keep drawing on them the way he draws on O'Hara. It makes sense. It would be some kind of anchor. I'm tired of drifting aimlessly. I envy Ted his Frank O'Hara, his inspiration. ("It's all there, I don't need anything else.")

I think I'm ready to come to terms with myself as an artist. To make some decisions and take a position based on an honest evaluation of who I am, what I have, what I can do (and what I *cannot* probably do). I think I am ready, if need be, to accept myself as an eccentric, or even a conservative who may never be in the vanguard of artistic thought. The important thing is to be able to work in a way that uses all my abilities hard — a way in which I can grow and learn and have and show Joy. I've been sitting around too long reading *Artforum* about everybody else. Now *me*.

2/22/70

Notes of conversation with Ted:

Have I ever examined my works as coming after Cubism? (First reaction — thinking about Cubism, etc. (what followed) has taken artists through surface, object and right off the canvas. I'm afraid to think about this because I want the option of working on canvas, but actually I *should* think about it since I obviously can't decide whether I want to work on canvas or not. (It may be that an exploration of my relation to Cubism is just what is missing from my experience.)

2/23/70

Washington's Birthday. No work.

Took mescaline and then an up pill yesterday, stayed up til 4:00 or 5:00 A.M. with Ted and Bill Berkson and Clark Coolidge (whom I just met and whom I like a lot).

Felt mostly pretty weird and frustrated on the mescaline because all we did was go across the street to George and Katie Schneeman's and sit around. I kept wanting to laugh a lot, felt very tense, like doing things and there was not much to do. Felt jealous of George because he was doing works with Ted and I wanted to work or do *something* and wasn't.

Later, home with Ted I gave him a long backrub and we joked and talked a lot and had a milkshake and later after taking part of a pill we talked some about making art (Ted says he hasn't written anything here yet — it's about time) and then we talked some about my art, like the question about relating myself to Cubism. (Ted says every major artist since Cubism has been aware of Cubism and considered it in his works.) And I shall too, I don't know *why* I've waited so long to confront that issue. Confronting it is the answer to my deciding about the formal problems in my work. Canvas or not? Paint or not? Sculpture? Environment? Stain? Brush? Ted said he knew he'd never say anything I wouldn't understand. That's just a nice thing to know.

Said that my car painting is nice but a little cerebral. I said why do you say that? He said because it looks like your conception was way ahead of your technique. True. Technique (with paint) is a problem for me.

One very interesting thought Ted asked me if I ever worked with confusion (like say, de Kooning). I said no, I always had to have thought through that and had to know, when I started a work, what I wanted. (I suspect this is because of my limited technique, partly.) He suggested one way to work (he said it was more *real life* — which sounds right) was to show the confusion stage arriving at order. I always go from the point of order on.

2/26/70

Tuesday night, Ted wasn't in the apartment when I got home, but later he came in and said he'd waited for me to come home after work but when I hadn't, he'd gone out (played pool with Jim Carroll and taken heroin and gotten sick). But I thought it was great he'd waited for me. He asked me what I'd done at the loft and I said I was reading about Cubism. And then he said he'd been thinking we'd had a great conversation about art the other night (Sunday) when he'd asked me if I'd thought of myself in relation to Cubism. Then he told me how he'd made a great study of Cubism and how *The Sonnets* were Cubistic. He told me about some of the books he'd read about Cubism, said the Skira book was pretty good and that Daniel-Henry Kahnweiler had written a really wonderful book about Juan Gris. And then we went on to talk about his works and my works and our ways of working — natural symbolism, "exhausting poetics" in any one series and other things. It was a great talk . . .

Mark Rothko was found dead yesterday in his studio, his wrists slashed. He was sixty-six.

At work (Paul Bacon Studio) I'm now reading Guy Habasque (Skira) on Cubism.

3/5/70

Ted came back from Providence last night after I'd decided he'd probably go to Yale first and get back here on Thursday. Well, it's wonderful to have him back. I'd brought home the Red Auerbach book so he read that straight through and laughed a lot and said it was terrific. He kept telling me little anecdotes about Red when I looked up to see what was so funny, like the "weeping towel" and then the time he went to the game and it began to rain and one team was losing so they wanted the game to be called off because of the rain but the umpire kept the game going so the next member of the losing team went up to bat wearing a giant rain coat . . . I was terribly sleepy after taking two muscle relaxers . . . we tried to sleep for awhile, but after having two *very* real dreams . . . I woke up to find Ted hadn't been able to fall asleep yet so we turned the light on and looked at all the reproductions in the *Cubism and the Twentieth Century Art* book. Ted discovered that it had no Picabias.

At about 5:00 A.M. I went back to sleep until the alarm rang at 8:00 when I got up (still feeling very relaxed in the muscles) and went to work. A great sunny warm spring morning.

3/9/70

Stayed home from work today to sleep. Ted is still sleeping now at 10:15 P.M. I slept til 2:00 or so this afternoon but couldn't sleep any more after that. Had LSD (a little) last night for the second time. Began to feel very high maybe an hour later. Went with Ted and Bill Berkson to see the movie of Henry Miller's *Tropic of Cancer*. By the time we got to the movie I was completely high in a combination mescaline-alcohol-amphetamine way. My teeth felt "itchy," my face felt twitchy like I wanted to laugh all the time, and I *did* feel giggly and somewhat uncoordinated. The taxi ride up to 59th Street was fast and terrific and the speed seemed very compatible with the LSD . . . The movie was *terrific*. It was set in Paris and I was completely involved. I couldn't believe when it was over . . . Afterwards we walked a couple of blocks (Ted wanted to go to Times Square) but it was very cold and windy, though I didn't feel any discomfort from the cold, so we took a cab to Max's where we walked through to sit in the red-lit room in the back (where apparently all the queens hang out). The room had an incredible glow and the people in it created a Satyricon kind of carnival. One of the waiters was a fantastic, graceful, monkey-looking creature with a face a lot like the face on the upper-right-hand figure in Picasso's *Demoiselles*. Long, gangling arms, agile form. He (she?) wore a wide, diamond-studded belt low and a scarf around long wispy-wild black hair. We just sat and watched and talked a little and had things like Bloody Marys and salad and mushrooms. After awhile we walked back to the apartment which looked cold and stark and harsh to me. Jim Carroll was there watching TV and nodding out. The nodding out scared me some. The apartment, too, appeared sort of dirty and ugly to me and soon I was washing the dinner dishes so that I would feel more comfortable. When I'd finished that, and Jim left, Ted and I finished watching the movie, a World War II film, on the bed, under the covers . . .

3/17/70
Ted has gone to Michigan and Iowa for two weeks. He left on Sunday . . . While Ted is away I am drawing self-portraits from the mirror in the apartment. This is in preparation for some portrait paintings I want to do. I really feel that I am on the right track. Ted helped. I can't remember just how he said it, but the idea was that you can still make great art with paint, but you won't make the cover of *Artforum*. It's a matter of whether you want to make lots of money and become internationally famous, or . . . I simply realized that I want to feel great about *making* my works. Being famous *that* way really doesn't matter to me one whit. I do believe that people like Alan Saret and Sonnier are making great art but so much thinking and so little doing is not for me. And so I've decided to paint again . . . also, even if I end up being a revolutionary new media artist it will have to evolve through and out of paint and out of really knowing paint. Evolve *through my hands*, intuitively and not in my head (or at least not so much in my head). I know that I can work hard and long and push myself harder with paint or pen, and that is what I really want to do now. Work *hard*. Push *through*. Later, at dinner with Ted and Joe Brainard, Joe voiced some doubts about paint but said that he wouldn't give it up for anything in the world. Ted turned to me and said, "You feel that way, too." And I smiled inside and said, "I know, I've made a little decision."

I've also been thinking that making art for me and for an audience of people I love and like, like Ted, is perhaps the only way that really makes sense. Why worry about some vague art public or even artists you read about in *Artforum* though you do think their works are great?

Anyway, you'll get there.

Talking, me complaining about never learning to draw and now having such a handicap, Ted says, "We always get into this argument, but I don't know why. *I believe in you.*"

Ted talking to Joe about Frank and how he was a great man. Ted saying that what he wants to do all the time is be a great man (though he says he'll never be as great a person as Frank) and write poetry that shows that he is a great man.

4/5/70

Wednesday, there was a great reading at the Church. Anne and Joe. Joe read his "I Remember" work. Ted said, "You could write like that too. It would be great."

4/7/70

Worked all day on mechanicals for which I will be paid $100. Never got to go outside and it was a bright sunny spring day, so I feel I missed something.

This morning was wonderful, though. Ted came back from spending some hours at the loft and woke me up to tell me he'd done something to my big sea horizon print. He said it looked great. The sun was streaming in the window.

I got up and showered and then looked at what he'd done to the print. It *was* pretty great. He'd pasted a picture (photo) of Duchamp's *Glass* on the blue part of the print and above it he'd written MONEY in black that ended in the black to the right.

We looked at it and talked about it and then I made scrambled eggs and toast and coffee . . . Afterward we signed our names to the collaboration and decided it should have a big silver frame. We'll hang it over the fireplace . . .

4/12/70

. . . to continue from 4/7/70: Ted called up from Bill's and said he was very high on a drug for amputees and did I want to come over. I said no, but later called him back and said I'd changed my mind.

For awhile Ted and I were alone at Bill's, then Larry Fagin came over. I looked at a Leonardo book and a Max Ernst book. I noticed in Leonardo how big the figure of the Mona Lisa is against the landscape. Yet still a part of the landscape. In the Max Ernst book I especially remember a rather Magritte-like work called *Night and Day*. Ted said he was more stoned than he'd been in years.

We went home about 1:30, on the way picking up some desk cubby holes from a desk abandoned on the street, buying a *Times* and running into Dick Gallup and Tom Veitch. When we got home Ted wanted: 1. a milk shake, 2. toast, 3. noodles.

4/17/70

Ted calls the new Japanese 150-watt lantern I put up over the bed, The Sun. "Let's turn on the Sun."

5/15/70

Quite depressed today . . . I feel terrible from not working. I am not really myself.

I'm afraid that Ted may be disappointed in me. I feel I'm coming off as a kind of a jerk because without my work, I have no place, no position, from which to speak, think, experience. And so I must begin to work NOW. To continue not to work will be terribly destructive.

This spring is drawing quickly to a close and I am beginning to feel anxious about missing Ted. At one time he said he might be "right here" in the fall. "Right here" being my bed. Now I don't know. We don't seem to be having such a glorious time right now . . . I'm afraid taking the acid with Ted out in Rye has changed things. I felt exposed there in a way I kept telling myself was not true . . . I should remember how I felt on the acid trip—when it felt good—when I got outside away from the house. I felt like an incredible creature—in an incredible, maybe prehistoric world—all new and alive and chirping, spinning, humming, brave. I remember how the tulip leaves looked, prehistoric, tropical, I remember the sun. Warm, I remember looking way across the swamp to a group of weeping willows. They were waving, vibrating in the wind. Everything was new green and rich deep earth. I said to Ted, "It's spring!" I remember how the stream looked low and streamlined, moving smoothly and I remember saying it used to be higher. And Ted said it probably just *looks* that way. And I felt the difference between standing there as a little girl and now as a proud tall woman. I remember leaves, branches, the ends of growing things calling to me with great spinning vibrations. I remember feeling sinister in a clean beautiful bright green, flashing-black way—like a priestess, like nature. Life and I were in collusion in a violent, beautiful, awesome, fearful secret. I felt bright, birdlike, powerful, evil and smiling. I felt like a kind of bird-dinosaur looking out surveying his world all alive and bright and powerful and clean and awesome like himself. Later, I wondered if I looked different to other people, maybe scary and Ted said, "No, except that now you have *power*."

I remember also a sinister, bright dark California kind of feeling — sunglasses and shiny powerful humming cars. And I remember a Jacques Tati feeling "Sunday afternoon in the country." "Great White America" said Ted.

I remember turning on to the putt-putt sounds of kiddie cars and traffic sweeping by and everything jumping and humming and friendly. I remember Ted saying then, "Now you're tripping. This is what it's like. You'll feel this way now for four or five hours"

Up on top!

Clean and moving cleanly ahead.

7/6/70

Found a special delivery letter waiting on the step for me from Ted: "Just a quick note: The drawings and your letter were beautiful. I'll call you this week. Here's telephone bill and other★. Love Ted."

★ $90.00 money order

7/26/70

. . . In the past week I've felt I've really come to understand what Ted was trying to tell me last year. That art is about all your feelings, not just the great ecstatic moment. All your life and feelings have value. I thought this as Ted lay in my bed and I was not happy and he was not happy but it was *real life* — my life. What I mean to say is, I think I'm ready to make great mature real works — in a steady strong way. No longer the high thin ecstatic dreaming way of working that worked so rarely. Now it's everything . . .

10/19/70

. . . Went to John Giorno's party at Gotham Book Mart and Ted comes in with a birthday present for me *One Hundred Years of Solitude* by Gabriel Garcia Marquez and *Scenes Along the Road*, photos of Kerouac, Ginsberg, Orlovsky, etc.

15. Flyer by Donna Dennis for a reading, April, 1971.

4/14/71

Last night I made a nice announcement for Ted's reading on Sunday . . . I drank a lot of wine and made a great, messy, starry constellation white on black work. A chair (Ted's chair) with his name above and stars wheeling all around. I like it a lot and it's perhaps the loosest work I've done yet . . . Ted never came to get the work. Called tonight and said he was sick and unfortunately we'd have to forget about printing up the announcement since there was no longer enough time to get it out. I was angry and disappointed . . .

5/26/71

. . . Working on an alternate design for *Memorial Day* just because I still have an early unfinished version around . . .

5/31/71 (Memorial Day)

Started (maybe finished) a work today called *Memorial Day* (working on a discarded version of the cover for Anne and Ted — for their work).

6/6/71

Worked from 1:00 A.M. to 4:00 A.M. this morning. I may have finished *Memorial Day*. Anyway, I've finished three small works in the last month . . . I think of Ted. Wonder where he is, when I'll see him again.

6/7/71

. . . I miss Ted. Wonder at moments if I'll see him again. Rosemary thinks he's the first friend who will die, too. Well, I still love Ted. Now he's inspiration. "I've never been interested in anyone who wasn't my equal," he said.

7/18/71

Valerie and Rob Hollister bought a work from me for $100 this weekend. The *Memorial Day* work. I'd been half thinking of sending it to Ted . . . It has so much to do with him. Came so much from the warmth of seeing him last time . . . I do feel that *Memorial Day* is my best work to date.

16. Proposed cover by Donna Dennis for *Memorial Day*, by Anne Waldman and Ted Berrigan, 1971.

10/19/79

Done some thumbnail sketches for the jacket of Ted's book *So Going Around Cities*. Hard. Thought I'd do the view out my window. Get drunk and just go on and on until it was done and the sun came up. But I'm not into abusing myself that way anymore and the wine tastes bad and I want this to be good . . . Guess this will take several nights. I'm apparently more and more of a sculptor and less and less a painter and it gets scarier to do something like this. Also my relationship with Ted has changed so much. I need to ponder that a bit too, I suppose . . . The feelings have mellowed a lot since he last asked me to do art for him.

3/16/80 3:00 A.M.

Ted left a couple of hours ago. We talked — terrifically — four or five hours. I enjoyed it tremendously. We can really talk now. He loves the new piece, *Tunnel Tower*. Can't remember just how he said it but my impression was he felt this piece *gave* more, right away. I'm tired! Wish I could remember it all. He felt *Two Stories with Porch* was the spookiest work of all time. Completely inviting from one angle, and then . . . VACANCY.

9/10/80

. . . As Ted said, the last two works *Two Stories with Porch* and *Tunnel Tower* are the ones that matter because before I was trying to deal with death (mastabas, grave houses, etc.) but with those two works, I already *knew* death, understood death.

10/7/82 (Postcard from Ted)

Dear Donna, If you miss this one, I'll kill you, personally, with my own bare little hands. Ron and I haven't read together, head to head, just the two of us, in NYC in ten years. We are going to show what it is we artists do and why we do it and what happens, what *it all means* and *what* the *only possible* result ever can be. And I'm going to shoot down Ron, one half of my self, like a dog in the dirt, while everyone laughs and has a great time (he'll get over it) and then I am going to curse God and die, almost, of light-headedness, and leave this world of Maya forever and go become a ride at Disneyland. (Love, Ted)

7/5/83 10:00 A.M.

Rosemary [Mayer] called me half an hour ago to say Ted has died. Ted is dead. *Ted Berrigan is dead*. Dead. Never more. I'm having a hard time trying to absorb it.

But as I write here, it's beginning to come. As I write here (or as I wrote above) I found myself reflexively wondering how this writing would read to someone who writes well. How would this page look, published. I think of how my journals, bits and pieces are beginning to be published and I realize that the greatest pleasure to come from that would have been to hear what Ted had to say. This makes me realize that in a deep-in-the-heart way, Ted has remained my mentor all these years. His was the opinion I cared most about. I'm talking about my art now. He did, finally, come to my show with his daughter, Kate, and wrote in the book, "Enthralling!" and, I think, forged Rauschenberg's signature under Kate's name. A very "Ted" kind of joke. "Mr. Bob Rauschenberg." I'll never know what he meant.

I would not be the artist I am without Ted. As simple as that. He believed in me before anyone else did and said so. He was at times almost unbearably difficult and then so generous. The generosity. He gave. And I will carry that with me always and pass it on, I hope, to others. I learned that from him, too. It will take me a long time to understand all I have from him in me. Mostly, I remember just now what Ted said of death. How when someone dies they pass from the outside to the inside and that is what I am trying to do now, find enough room inside to put all I knew as Ted.

—Donna Dennis

17. "Back when, circa '63–'64: we were crawling out of the salt and slag of the lower east side. The mercury shimmered between heartbeats, cheap rooms and pirogi. Four poets in search of a publisher . . . Berrigan, Brodey, Katzman and Sanders."

— Allen Katzman

PART TWO

A Religious Experience

I was looking at the words he
was saying . . . like . . . Okinawa . . .
bandage . . . real . . . and suddenly
I realized I had read somewhere that,
"in their language the word for 'idiot'
is also the word meaning 'to breathe through
your mouth.' "And I was simply left there
in bed, being looked at.

— Ted Berrigan

New York Diary 1967

LEWIS WARSH

October 31

The alarm rings: it's 2:00 P.M. I get up, dress & go downstairs to buy the *Post*. It's Halloween. Call the typewriter repair shop & learn that it will cost $25 to have my typewriter repaired. Read a few chapters from *A Confederate General from Big Sur*. Anne returns. I go out, take some packages to the post office on 14th Street. Then I go to the library around the corner. I get a new library card but there are no books I want to take out. Take more packages to the P.O. on 4th Avenue. Return home; it's almost dark out. Anne comes home. Peter comes by. We talk about Peter Viereck who is going to read at St. Mark's. Anne cooks dinner. Peter leaves. I re-write part of an old poem on Anne's typewriter. At about 9:00 I go to the church to the reading which started at 8:30. Meet Shelly at door to the church. She's going to a big Halloween party at the Village Theater. Reading has not yet started. There aren't many people there: Anne & Ted & Larry & Peter. After the first set I leave. It's Halloween. Kids are running through the street asking people for money. In front of Gem Spa I meet Katie & Debbie & their kids. There are three cops on the corner. We all go upstairs. I give the kids all the Halloween candy which Anne brought home during the day. Also, I give Katie "Big Lew," the robot Larry bought on Avenue C. Just as they're leaving Larry arrives. Also, Shelly. Larry just found an apartment on 86th Street. Sandy calls. She's coming over with David & Kate. Katie, Debbie & the kids leave. Sandy arrives. Shelly leaves to return to the Halloween party at the Village Theater. Jim calls. Anne & Ted arrive, home from the reading. David falls asleep in my arms on the couch. Shelly returns. The party is obviously dragging. Jim arrives. He needs to use Anne's typewriter to type poems. Wren comes. Ted, Sandy & the kids leave. Anne cooks me a hamburger. Shelly leaves. Wren leaves. Jim is still typing. Ron & Pat leave. Jim & I go downstairs to Gem Spa to get ice cream. Jim buys a copy of the new *Downbeat*. Anne makes us ice cream sodas. Lee and a friend of his named Jeff arrive. Jim begins falling asleep. I explain reasons why he can't sleep over on couch. He calls his girlfriend & secures a place to stay. Lee & Jeff leave. Jeff says he will call tomorrow to show us his poems. We discuss everything & everybody with Jim. Ted arrives. He has a copy of *The Sonnets* which neither Anne nor Jim has seen. Jim leaves. I read the newspaper, Ted speed-reads *Freewheelin' Frank*, Anne reads *The Sonnets*. Then Ted leaves.

November 1

Set the alarm for 10:00 A.M. but wake instead at 1:00. While having breakfast Harris calls. Anne speaks to him first, then I do. He plans to stay in NY, find a job, his own apartment, etc. Make plans to see him the next day. Then Anne goes out. Finish *A Confederate General from Big Sur*. Walk down 8th Street to 8th Street Bookstore. Ted's *Sonnets* is in the store as well as Paul Blackburn's *The Cities*. Note error in table of contents in Blackburn's book. Buy the *Post* and the *Voice*. Both boring. Read about rebellious CCNY students. Knicks lose 6th in a row. Then Anne comes home. We address & paste stamps on the announcement Bill Beckman made for reading she & Jim are giving at St. Mark's next week. While we are doing this Ted arrives. He & Sandy were to have dinner at Steve Holden's, but Sandy must baby-sit. I decide to go up to Steve's with Ted. Anne has to go to the church for a reading of Greek poets. First, Ted & I walk to 8th Street Bookstore to get a copy of *The Sonnets* to give Steve. There is rain in the air. We take a cab to Steve's on East 74th Street. Steve has hundreds of old & current 45s, & most of the old ones are terrific. Among them: "Tragedy" by Thomas Wayne, "Hey Girl" by Freddie Scott, & many others. I discover a record written by Steve Holden. It's by Rod McKuen. It came out in 1959. We eat chicken, rice. Drink wine. Eat ice cream. Discuss poetry. Play more records. Read Steve's poetry. Discuss poetry conference at Berkeley & Ted's reading there, which Anne & I were present at (though we didn't really know Ted). Listen to more music. Then we leave. It's raining. We walk downtown for awhile. It's 11:00 P.M. Then we take a cab to my house. Anne isn't there. She probably went somewhere after the reading. We go over to Ron's. He isn't home. We try calling Peter but all the phone booths on 2nd Avenue have been vandalized. Then we meet Tom Veitch and Richard Kostelanetz. Richard leaves. I go into a candy store & call Peter's; no one is home. Tom, Ted & I start back to Ron's where Tom is staying. On the way we meet Anne. Reading lasted a long time & she was coming from the church. We all go to Ron's. Ron says he was in the bathroom when we came by before. Tessie & Pat have gone to Tulsa. After awhile Anne gets hungry. Ted, Anne & I leave. At Gem Spa we meet Erroll & Julian. I see somebody who I know I've seen somewhere before. He's eating an ice cream cone & a candy bar. We smile at each other. I say: "Where have I met you?" He says: "There." Ted goes home. Anne & I go home. As we walk upstairs I look behind me & see the person I spoke to lurking outside the building. Anne eats at home. A few minutes later Peter & Linda arrive. Everybody's fading out in their own way. I think about Tom Clark & what he's been doing. Then Peter & Linda leave. I wish I had a typewriter.

18. Tom Clark, Ted Berrigan and Ron Padgett, circa 1968.

November 2

I wake up early, 11:00 A.M. Peter comes by. He has been awake all night on pills.
Then Anne gets up, has breakfast, goes to work. Peter leaves too. Then Harris
arrives. He is very quiet; doesn't want to talk about Rochester or anything else.
We go out, first to Tompkins Square Bookstore (walking through the park) but
it's closed, then to the post office, then to Tom Clark's. Harris still not opening
up very much. At 5:00 Tom, Harry & I walk back across town in the rain. Tom
goes to see Peter. Harris & I go home. Anne is home. She's making supper since
Simone is supposed to come at about 7:00. Harris has to leave to see his mother
who is in a hospital uptown. I'm getting tired when Simone comes. Spend
intervening time reading *Franz Kline: An Emotional Memoir* by Fielding Daw-
son. Then Tom arrives & the four of us eat supper. After supper we sit around
talking. George Kimball arrives, stays for awhile, then leaves. Then Larry
arrives. Then Martha. We decide to go to the movies, to see *Cool Hand Luke.* It's
playing uptown. Anne, Simone & I take one cab; Larry, Martha & Tom
another. The movie is pretty good. Afterwards, Simone gets a cab & goes
home. Tom, Martha & Larry get another cab. Anne & I walk to 2nd Avenue
and get a bus going downtown. The bell downstairs just rang a few times but
we didn't answer it.

November 3

Ted calls early in the afternoon and later comes over with Kate. Jim comes by. He brings me a birthday present, a record by Arlo Guthrie. Anne goes to the church. Ted, Jim, Kate & I go downtown, to Delancey Street, to get pills (obetrols) with fake prescription which Ted has. While waiting for the pills we go into Ratner's on Delancey Street. Drugstore refuses to fill the prescription. Walk back to Avenue C. Ted & Kate go home. I go to drugstore on Avenue C where they fill the prescription. Walk up to 9th Street with Jim. Jim goes to Bill's & I go home. Anne, at home, tells me that we've been invited to a party Les Levine is giving that night. At about 8:30 we go down to Ted's workshop at the courthouse. Meet Dick & Peter & Ron Zimardi. Peter says that Sandy called to say that Ted is sick, that the workshop will be called off. Dick, Ron, Anne & I go to Peter's. Carol, Crissie & Linda are there, watching TV. Dick & Peter play chess. Anne & I read. Soon Ron leaves. Then Dick & Carol & Crissie go home & we go to the party. On the Bowery we see a man lying in the street totally naked. There are only a few people at the party when we arrive. We talk with John Perreault. I don't know anyone else who is there. I don't feel like drinking. I feel terrific waves of energy & restlessness at everything being so static. More people start coming in. Sandy & Lee arrive. I talk to Sandy for awhile. Then we start dancing. Sweat drips down my face, but I feel good. At about 1:00, Anne & I leave & return home.

November 4

Saturday afternoon; time I hate the most. Never want to get out of bed. Sandy calls. I try to get tickets for *The Beard* but they're too expensive. At about 4:00, Anne & I go over to Bill's. Sandy is baby-sitting there. Bill & Jim are there too. (Before this, Ted, Larry & Joan came over to our place, stayed for awhile then returned to Ted's.) Sandy, Anne, Kate, David & I go back to Ted's. First I take Kate back. Ted, Joan & Larry are listening to tapes. Everybody will have dinner there. After dinner Larry & Joan go uptown to Radio City Music Hall. At about 9:00, Ted, Anne & I leave & walk across town. We go into the record store on St. Mark's Place where I buy "Different Drum" by the Stone Ponies & "Don't Worry Baby" by the Beach Boys. Outside our apartment we meet Lee, Dick & Carol. They're going to the movies on 42nd Street. First they come upstairs & for about an hour we listen to records. Martha comes over with her typewriter since mine is still being repaired. We all decide to go uptown to the movies. On

19. Ted Berrigan, Jim Carroll, Lee Crabtree and Julius Orlovsky at Allen Ginsberg's farmhouse in Cherry Valley, New York, 1969.

42nd Street we see *The Counterfeit Traitor* with William Holden. It isn't bad. It's getting cold out. We can't find a cab. Dick & Carol & Lee fade out. We take the BMT back to St. Mark's Place. It's 2:30 A.M. We sit around, have coffee. Ted walks Martha home. I go out for the newspaper. There is nothing interesting in it to read.

—Lewis Warsh

On Your Birthday

LARRY FAGIN

David said I want my mommy to make the cake and I like devil cakes.
Do not let all this emotion upset you Ted.
Don't cry.
Don't laugh either.
It's not funny to turn 33 (turn it you still get 33)
It's in the cards for fellows like you to drift along. Sabe?
Then begins a life of struggle and penury, but also discovery.
But 33 what? you may well ask, having no sense of time.
Well, your beard is not like grass because small animals do not pee there.
Your beard is like time.
That's not bad!
It's meaningless.
A beard should not mean but be.
Now your babies may cry but they are firm.
It is nice for you to be their father.
You are really nice.
People like and enjoy you
Both on stage and in person.
So you finish first, you see, just like Goethe predicted you would!
Ted, you don't need a pension
You need a regular payment, not a fee, given to artists, etc., by
　　their benefactors; subsidy. In France and other continental
　　countries, a boarding school or boarding house.
Here in your house it's nice to be
At 11:15 in New York City.
Night and day it will always be
11:15 in New York City
In your brains
In your beard
In the bosom of your home
In a hole at the bottom of the sea.

1967

Awake on March 27th

KENWARD ELMSLIE

my thoughts turn up
always the first one up around here
Ted's god-fearing farmer red Hi Folks beard
with its growth of unabashed pseudo-pubic hair
mebbe's scratching kinkily against the clean maiden
sheets as pellets of old speed sift through his system
asleep on top floor

yesterday empty excursion bus parked outside
babble babble ma and pa duck pat of butter daily
twenty years problem of month adds 165 pounds

Missing Persons to your Easter weight Easter weight
in place of street space a wall of bus windows
scary to come downstairs staring into bus

empty motor running empty stretched out on backseat
man face up corpse-gray uniform
end of sleepers list

1970

This is Happy Birthday to You Ted

JOANNE KYGER

Like so many names
In our Game
It adds up
I saw a seal head come up
Why am I not, Why am I not
I wish you a house in order

Change

for Ted

ROBERT CREELEY

Turning—
One wants it all—
No
Defenses.

1:31P.M. June 5th 1970

for Ted Berrigan

TOM RAWORTH

my up
is mind made

absolutely empty

now here comes thought thought
is laughing at language language
doesn't see the joke the joke
wonders why it takes so long

but it's friday
and it's a long way down

Chicago

TOM RAWORTH

pistol whipcracks i wondered about
are ted typing below

white snow

Tom Clark Interviews Ted Berrigan

TOM CLARK: First, how would you put together a sentence, if you were the master of all time and space?

TED BERRIGAN: How would I put together a sentence? Let me think. I guess I would just do it the same way I do now, I would just open my mouth and pop it out. And I would be listening to it while it came out. Sometimes I hear my words before they get to my lips, and if I don't like them I change them before they get out. But the only change I usually know how to make is, if I don't like a word, I only know how to change it to the opposite of what it means. So that that really limits me in a certain way in my poems. But, you know, like I'll change the noun or the verb to the exact opposite of what it means if I don't like what it says. I have the total Hegelian dialectic sense of doing things either this or that.

TC: In your works, what is the place of the tiny man in the back of the head?

TB: Well, he takes care of the measure. And he takes care of setting up the rhymes so that, at the point when I get to hear them, just before they come out, they're in the right place. That right place being the place in conjunction with all my theories which I've developed over the years, which include all theories. That is that sometimes they should be totally off-rhymes like Lewis MacAdams does them, where he puts a rhyme and then at the place where it should fall next according to the musical sequence, instead he puts it sort of the word before. Do you understand that? So you don't really notice rhymes in his poems when you're reading them for sense, then when you hear him read them you notice that they keep falling . . . In that poem that he and I wrote together[1] we wrote in exactly the same manner, but my rhymes all fall on the exact place in the most middle-of-the-road manner, whereas his are all either slightly before or slightly after. So, depending on what kind of poem I'm doing then the little man takes care of those rhymes too. So that if I'm doing a poem like "Peace," which I meant to be an absolute straightforward poem like a John Sebastian song, then the rhymes fell in the exact middle-of-the-road place. But if I'm doing a different kind of poem, like "Corridors of Blood"[2] or "Presence."[3] "Presence" is a good example, the rhyming words fall helter skelter throughout. So you get these sounds popping up here and there, but they're dissonant with the sense. So he takes care of that. And let me see if there's anything else that he does, actually . . . I mean, he's done that, that's been taken care of. I always loved rhyme. Edgar Allen Poe was a great favorite of mine, and Conrad Aiken in a certain way, and Eliot. I guess I was always influenced by the way Eliot uses rhyme, when I read it as an American.

TC: Like *The Four Quartets* or something.

TB: Yeah, or . . . No, like *The Preludes*. Or also like Milton's *Lycidas*, where when I read it with my not-so-good diction, the rhymes fall at uneven places. Whereas when I hear it read in good English, English-English, with good diction, the rhymes fall more evenly I noticed. But, I mean, I hear it back and forth, you know. I always did it that way until I got into Yeats, when I was teaching, and somehow I didn't give it any thought. But the little man must've thought about it, because then I started . . .

TC: It's like in "Peace." [4]

TB: . . . using . . . Yeah, in "Peace" was like the big influence.

TC: I think that in the works like "Peace" and in the *Buffalo Stamps* collaboration with Lewis MacAdams you were just talking about, the rhymes make the works like lullabies.

TB: Fast lullabies.

TC: I mean, they seem related to the rhythms of sleep, as opposed to . . . Like, in "Presence" the rhymes are jerky and they're related to awakeness rhythm, but in . . .

TB: Right. There's a go-get'em attitude in "Presence" and those other ones. Whereas in this one there's a lilt. It's a lilt. And it is related to sleep but in a funny way because it's also related to speed. That poem was the shoot'em-up poem. We both shot up that day and wrote that.

TC: Do you think that rhymes and puns work the same way?

TB: Yeah, but puns are a little trickier on the one hand, which I don't really care for too much because I'm not really clever. I mean, when I do a pun I always have to sort of burlesque it. I can't slip puns over too quickly. They get telegraphed, like you telegraph a punch. So I always burlesque it a little. But on the other hand, puns have a beautiful . . . They're like a one-two. Whereas a rhyme is like a connection, with the one up here and the two down here, and they flow more. But they are very similar I think. And also you can do so many things with rhymes. I mean, you can do the beautiful off-rhymes, and you can rhyme a word like "there," which is one of my favorite words to rhyme. "There." I like the way it sounds, like in "And I was there and I was there."[5] Then you can rhyme it with the middle syllable of another word in the next line and stuff. And that's what I really like to do. I mean, I'm into Natural Numbers, like Rexroth talks about. But I mean, he regards it as some count. But I don't count. With me it's really natural. But I mean, where I do count is I know where the rhyme should fall and then I either let it fall there, or I hit it a couple of steps sooner, or I hit it a little bit after, or else I don't do it at all. And sometimes when I don't do it at all, I do it at the end of the next unit of speech that's the same length as those, or at the end of half of that. You know what I mean? I think I really write in units of speech and half units.

TC: Phrases.

TB: Yeah, like phrases. Right. And to me there'd be like two phrases usually, or sometimes three. Two or three.

TC: The rhymes fall on the phrases instead of the lines. They fall at the ends of the phrases.

TB: Right. And sometimes I jump a phrase.

TC: There's one section where there's about twelve rhymes in about five lines, in long lines and there's lines within the lines, like phrase-lines.

TB: Right. Sometimes that's the way I can do. Just like in *The Sonnets* [6] there's the phrases as played against the length of the line. But the lines are long in that poem. But I mean, in the phrases it'd be like one two three maybe.

TC: So then if you open it . . .

TB: Sometimes I'll hit every one two three with a rhyme.

TC: Well, like when you go from *The Sonnets* into the poems with open space, then you're just breaking the sonnet line of, say, three phrases up into three different lines with a phrase in each line.

TB: Yeah, except I'm not breaking it up. I'm allowing them more of their own. I'm not charging. I'm laying back a little. So, when you lay back a little, the equivalent amount of space between the phrases becomes more vivid to you, more present. And so I let it be in there. That's what it is. It's like the difference between laying back and charging. And in *The Sonnets* I was charging. Like Arnold Palmer, you know . . . . The syntax ended at the end of the line. Thought in relation to syntax ends at the end of every line. Not *every* line, because I varied that. But in the open poems I'm sort of laying back and floating the lines up there instead of shooting them out onto the page.

TC: Well, that's like the rhyme thing I was talking about. It's like floating space where, instead of moving ahead, you stay turning around in the same space. And puns have the same effect of you're going ahead but you're also staying in the same place because you're spinning. You know what I mean? And rhymes do that too. They give this effect of spinning.

TB: Right. A slower more gentle spin, though, than puns. A little more gentle. I mean, the puns are quicker.

TC: I was thinking of that New Year's Resolution poem that ends "don't tread on me." You know, "thirty-three"?[7]

TB: "Don't you tread on me."

TC: Well, my mother-in-law was teaching that poem to nursery school students who totally loved it because the rhymes in it had the effect on them that the poetry that they dig had. In other words, simple but the rhyme giving it a singsong effect.

TB: Well, in those it does give it a singsong effect, but also it's pushed. I mean, I pushed the rhymes.

> I am 33. Good Wishes, brothers, everywhere,
> & Don't You Tread On Me.

Where, in this other poem I was into using more . . . What's the foot that has two unaccented syllables and an accented one?

TC: Alexandrine Trochee?

TB: Whatever it is, I wasn't using those consciously. I mean, thinking about that kind of foot. But I was into that kind of rhythm.

TC: I know what you mean. Right.

TB: It's like: up the stairs, into the room, across the floor.

TC: Do the job.

20. Ted Berrigan escorting Angelica Heinegg to her wedding at St. Mark's Church In-the-Bowery, 1968. Ted gave the bride away to Tom Clark.

TB: Sit at the chair. I mean, in all my poems I'm pushing. I mean, I'm pushy. But in that kind of poem, for example, I've found by using rhyme that I can get it to go like this instead of like that. Because in *The Sonnets* I was always going like that. But in the open poems I'm taking a cluster of about five words, not all on one line, and putting them up like blocks like Hans Hofmann. In fact that's what I'm influenced by, that push. Joe Brainard I got it from more or less, but it's that push–pull.

TC: That's interesting because in those rhymed works like "Peace," the feeling I got from it was of . . . two feelings, one of grace, and one of awkwardness at the same time. And the grace didn't come easy. And that's what I dug about it, because it was a stumbling grace. I mean, it was like a slightly falling forward, like just ahead of the beat or behind the beat.

TB: Yeah, that awkward grace.

TC: Like Edwin [Denby] talks about a sense of the beat, but then being a little ahead of it or a little behind it making it interesting.

TB: Right. Well, that awkward grace was like . . . I mean, it's there and I can use it, but it has to be the right poem. To show that I could use it.

TC: So, do you think the way you walk is related to the way you talk? I mean, that sense of the pistons in the poems seems like the way the poem walks. You know?

TB: That's right. Well, I used to walk and talk exactly the same way. And now I do that some of the time, but more often it's sort of slightly two different things. I mean, I talk faster than I walk now. Whereas I used to walk just as fast as I talk. And that was *The Sonnets*.

TC: Do you think that the famous 1966 ankle injury had some relation?

TB: Yeah, but it was also just a symbolic event for getting to be thirty years old.

TC: You know, it's interesting that walking seems to stimulate talking. I mean, you always can carry on a conversation in your head when you're walking. Like, when you're by yourself you seem to have one voice, but . . .

TB: Well, ninety percent of my poems come out of walking, taking walks.

TC: Right. Like "American Express"[8] and poems like that.

TB: Well, even the ones that are not about that. They come to me, and no matter where they come to me they usually get sort of worked out while I'm walking. And by worked out I mean, the poems come to me by getting a phrase or so and a big sense that I can do what I can do with it, which I cut off after the phrase. When I'm walking I allow myself to let a few phrases start coming together. I'll get a little cluster of lines here, a little cluster there. But I never let it work itself out. I always keep it all up in the air until I get to the typewriter, because I'm a total action-writer, you know . . .

TC: I read somewhere that Milton would take these walks every day with his daughter, who was like his scribe.

TB: His seeing-eye daughter.

TC: She would come with him and apparently she would bring notebooks and he would walk and he would work out the lines to his poems in his head, like, on *Paradise Lost* he would work out like sixty lines at a time in his head and then he would dictate sixty lines and he would always do it while he was walking. It seems incredible. You know, like, I can only usually carry about two lines.

TB: Right. But I guess if you're blind you must make a whole big adjustment. Because I think that we cut it off after not too many lines. I'm about the same as you. I cut it off after that, because if I really finish it I might never type it up. Because the physical reality of the typewriter makes it so tangible to me, and then I really do the things that I like to do. It gives it a weight like bricks. I mean really, I often think of my words as sort of bricks. But the bricks then are underneath the words, sort of. I use the words a lot of times to disguise the fact that it's a brick underneath, or to make the brick float. And then there'll be a key-word like a rhyme to put the brick right there.

TC: There's a line in *The Sonnets* that says . . .

TB: That's the best thing I've said in five years about my works actually.

TC: There's a line in *The Sonnets* that says "everything in this light turning into stones."

TB: "Everything in this light turning into stones." [9]

TC: Which is actually where I got the idea of naming that book *Stones*, you know.

TB: Oh, that's wonderful.

TC: And then Dick Gallup later told me that that was a line of his that you stole from him.

TB: Well, actually I changed it. I changed it.

TC: Well, it was great to have used it. He had "everything in this light turning into stones," or something like that. And then in *The Sonnets* it says . . .

TB: Mine says, "Everything in this light turning to stones," I think. And then the next line says, "ash bark like cork a fading dust."

TC: Well, I think it's who uses a line where it's used in context is great.

TB: Well, it does come from a line of Dick's, off a line of Dick's, but I don't even remember what Dick meant by the line. And I'm using it as an abstract line.

TC: I can only think about the meaning of that line as a line in *The Sonnets*.

TB: In Dick's poem it wasn't so good anyway. I mean, it had what's good about Dick's works in it, with a few quagmires at the beginning and end. And it's a poem he sort of threw out later. I mean, in fact it's a sort of ghastly poem that he threw out. But I took it and I rearranged a few lines, moved the things around, changed a couple of things. I mean, it was a sonnet which I made from all lines by him. There was no attempt to hide that it was all by him. And there's one other one I made from all lines by Ron [Padgett]. They come shortly afterwards. Because about the point where I got to those two, I wanted to check out my method by seeing if it could work on any sources besides my own old works. So I used Dick's, because I knew Dick's and Ron's poems all by heart. I was reading them all every day. I knew them all by heart.

TC: What's your favorite line in *The Sonnets?* I'll tell you what mine is.

TB: I suppose it would be "baffling combustions are everywhere."

TC: My favorite line in *The Sonnets* is "fucking is so lovely, who can say no to it afterwards."

TB: Yeah, well, in those . . . See, like, I don't really have favorite lines. I said that line because, for one thing, I made it all up completely. And for another thing, Ron told me he really loved it, and I'm very influenced by anything Ron likes.

TC: It's like a totally primordial line.

TB: Yeah. But I mean, usually my favorite lines are ones that I can read and deliver with a lot of feeling, and the "fucking is so very lovely who can say no to it later" I can really deliver. I deliver that with a certain kind of anger or bitterness, sort of. I mean, not heavy bitterness, not heavily bitter.

TC: Not heavily, not absurdly.

TB: I'm saying it to a girl.

TC: It's a totally tender line.

TB: Yeah, it's meant to be.

TC: It's like the word "fucking" is really hard to put in a tender context, because it has a social association.

TB: I was able to use that word at the beginning of the line and then take your attention off it incredibly without losing it, because I did this little spin, "who can say no to it later." It just goes along.

TC: That's the great thing about *The Sonnets*. It can contain lines long enough to put a total universe of thought in like that.

TB: I mean, I got away with everything I ever could have wanted to get away with in that work. I mean, if I could only write another book like that I'd love to. But it was a total method book, in that the media and the message . . . I mean, there is no such thing as a message and a media in the abstract. But I mean, they're the same thing to the perfect extent. That is, surpassing McLuhan where he says the message is the media. No. When it all works right there's no message, it's only sort of the media. Which is fascinating because of just the words. I mean, this house is made out of all the things it's made out of. In effect this house is nothing but the media, and everything in it.

TC: This is the message. I mean, the house is the message.

TB: Yeah. Well, what a funny thing to say. No message without the media.

TC: There's another question here that says, How does the message go from the head to the heart to the fingers, or vice versa?

TB: Well, that's a good question actually. But I'll say something before I answer it. To begin with, I always thought of each one of my poems, like *The Sonnets*, as being a room. And before that, I used to think of each stanza as being a room. And that each stanza should be a different room. And they should go like that, so that the space in between was that. So that when you got out of the room, you went sort of like that. You went just like that into the next room. But then *The Sonnets,* I made them to be a whole room. But then each line or each two lines or each three lines would be a part of the room, sort of. And then in the open poems, although it's also usually a room, instead of there being sections of the room, I was interested in the air. And I tried to have the poems go like that, around the room and move around. I tried to get it up.

TC: Like mobiles.

TB: Right. Sort of like mobiles but without the actual materials. Like a mobile made out of wind or something, you know? But for a non-moving thing, sort of a mobile is not a bad thing. The mobile would be somehow like a Tinguely machine, which would beat its head against the ice box once in a while, and drop on the floor over here and still somehow go back up in the air. That's sort of what mine are like. But that question, How does it go from the head to the heart to the fingers . . . Well, I guess the catalyst is a phrase or two. God knows where those come off of. Other books, other poems, something somebody says, things that have been in my head that had nothing to do with it and clicked together.

TC: So it seems to go from the head to the heart through the mouth to the fingers.

TB: No, it usually goes from the heart . . . I mean ideally, when it's working the best, something has happened which gives the heart that slightly heavy feeling, that is not really a downer, but that makes your blood sing. I'm talking about "Peace" now. It makes your blood sing in a certain way that the light is about five o'clock in the afternoon, or four o'clock in the afternoon in the fall when the shadows are long. It makes your heart sort of sing that way. A little bit slow, sort of. And then . . . It's a phrase, thought. You've got to have a phrase or two, and that involves a rhythm, a musical . . . A tune, almost, Yeats would say. A musical rhythm. And then where the fingers come in is when you have that rhythm, and the feeling is all really there in you, and you have a phrase or two, you have them in a way like being pregnant and about to have a baby. You have the whole rhythm and you sit down and you start coming out, you start typing. By the time I've typed up the phrases . . . or, if I don't want to use them at the beginning, I use one of my standard phrases, like what time it is and everything. But this one, I had one at the beginning. It was "what to do when the day's heavy heart." I mean, "heavy heart" was what I had right there. And by the time I got "what to do / when the day's heavy heart / having risen late / in the already darkening east," I mean, there was my music. That the fingers were dancing.

So Robert Duncan's right, I guess. It *is* a dance.

TC: That's beautiful. There's a question here that that's sort of the answer to, in a way, where it says, What kind of light do you like? and another one says, What colors do you like to use? I mean, in your works. What you said about five o'clock and light in the poems. But there's other ones.

TB: Yeah. I also like to use the famous light at 5:15 A.M. Like when the sun is sort of up, but it's only a quarter of the way up.

TC: Yeah. It's that rosy light.

TB: Yeah, well, it is. It's a magic light. I mean, it gives you an uncanny feeling as if it's really about three o'clock in the afternoon but there's nobody in the streets. It's that Sunday-afternoon-in-New-York-City feeling, in the midtown when nobody's there and you're walking around. It's sort of beautifully alone. And the loneliness you might feel comes as a sort of nostalgia for everybody that's in their houses and everything. But it really has to do with the light for me. Incidently, that I don't get in California much.

TC: Well, there seems like there's different lights. It's like there's one kind of light in certain guys. Like John Wieners, I always dig an electric light indoors at night, that the light is like a black and white that comes from an indoor late night. And then there's another kind of light that's like really a flat hot noon light which I dig in certain French guys. Like Ron has a hard sparkle in his works that seems like a certain noon. And California is a little more of that kind of light, you know . . . . And then Michael McClure has a great light that has blood in it for me. I always see this light with . . .

TB: Purple.

TC: Blood come through it.

TB: I see this incredible, like, neon.

TC: Purple, mauve.

TB: A certain kind of room where the shadow makes everything be purple.

TC: Dark brown. He has dark brown.

TB: Times Square. Sometimes a little bit like Times Square when you get out of the movies about four o'clock in the morning and the streets are a little sordid and everything. That's the kind of light I see in Mike McClure a lot.

TC: Like, Anne [Waldman] has this red white and blue light in her works, that's just starting to come in. Sort of ice cream.

TB: Like kindergarten ten o'clock in the morning light.

TC: But it's weird, because in Bob Creeley's works the only light I ever see is the white and the black of the words on the paper. I mean, I never see a room light or a space outdoor light.

TB: He probably writes in some room that gets somehow the indirect daylight, so that he doesn't see out any windows or anything when he gets total daylight in the room. But, Ann Arbor, you know, that's what made all the . . .

TC: It's a green leafy light. I dig that completely.

TB: That's what made all those poems like "Peace" and "Ann Arbor Song."[10] That's one of my most favorite poems, because I was able to be so corny, and yet I did in that poem practically everything I know how to do. I started in the middle of a poetry reading.

TC: Who was reading, actually?

TB: Some incredible jackoff. I don't really know. Somebody I didn't like. But I mean, I didn't like the works so much but I didn't actually dislike them. So I was getting these pleasant little riffs of my own. I was feeling sort of ok, you know? Sort of nice. Alice was at home in my house. And then suddenly this guy came over to me and said, Anne Waldman called you and she wants you to call back. And I said ok. And he started to walk away and then he turned around and said, she wanted to tell you Jack Kerouac is dead. Jesus, man, I felt like I got hit right in the head with a hammer. I went outside and I started crying. And Don Hall came over to me and said, what's the matter? He was very sympathetic. But, anyway, that light was very congenial to me. And I really got into a different kind of poem there. That light somehow gave me permission to be the age I was. I mean, I didn't have to be charging and therefore be younger and out ahead of myself. It gave me permission to be like a thirty-year-old ballplayer who had five more years to play, so wasn't thinking about retiring yet, but didn't have to be like a twenty-two-year-old anymore. And I started really writing my poems.

Bolinas 1971

Notes

1. "Home Free" by Ted Berrigan and Lewis MacAdams, published in *Buffalo Stamps*.
2. From *In The Early Morning Rain* by Ted Berrigan, Cape Goliard, 1970.
3. Ibid.
4. Ibid.
5. A line from Kenward Elmslie's poem "Expert at Veneers."
6. *The Sonnets*, Grove Press, 1968.
7. "Resolution" appears in *Many Happy Returns*, Corinth Books, 1968.
8. From *In the Early Morning Rain*.
9. Sonnet VI in *The Sonnets*.
10. From *In The Early Morning Rain*.

The Chicago Poem

for Ted Berrigan and Alice Notley

JEROME ROTHENBERG

the bridges of Chicago
are not the bridges of Paris
or the bridges of Amsterdam
except they are a definition
almost no one bothers to define
like life full of surprises
in what now looks to be the oldest
modern American city
o apparition of the movie version of
the future circa 1931
the bridges soon filled with moving lines
of people workers' armies
in the darkness of first December visit
along the water
bend of the Chicago River
the cliffs of architecture like palisades
at night the stars in windows
stars in the poem you wrote a sky
through which the el train pulls its lights
in New York streets of childhood
is like a necklace (necktie) in the language of
old poems old memories
old Fritz Lang visions of the night before
the revolution the poor souls
of working people we all love
fathers or uncles
lost to us in dreams & gauze
of intervening 1960s
there are whole tribes of Indians
somewhere inhabiting
a tunnel paradise
they will wait it out still
with a perfect assurance of things to come

everyone so well read in old novels
maybe the economics of disaster Ted
depressions of the spirit
so unlike the bright promise of
the early years
gloss of the young life easing death
atop a hill in Lawrence Kansas
the afternoon sky became aluminum
 (illumination)
played on a tambourine to calm
the serpent fear
the material corpse that leaves us vulnerable
everyone will come to it I think
I do not think you dig it
getting so out of hand so far away
but we remain & I will
make another visit soon
hope we can take a walk
together it is night & we are
not so bad off have turned forty
like poets happy with our sadness
we are still humans in a city overhung
with ancient bridges
you pop your pill I laugh
look back upon the future of
America & remember
when we both wrote our famous poems called
Modern Times

—Jerome Rothenberg

21. Merrill Gilfillan, Ted Berrigan and Alice Notley, 1969. Photo by Jayne Nodland.

"Sitting on the steps of the house on University Road where Frank O'Hara had rented a room to live in in 1950-1951 while a graduate student at the University of Michigan. Jayne Nodland took this photo in the Fall of 1969, where she & Merrill were living in Ann Arbor & I was teaching at the U. of Michigan. Alice was visiting from Iowa City. The house was empty & abandoned with radical political, hippie & profane graffiti all over. Given to me for my 46th birthday, 15 November 1980, from Jayne".

— Ted Berrigan

22. Alice Notley, Ted Berrigan and Pat Padgett in Southhampton, New York, 1970. Photo by Ron Padgett.

Desperately Awaiting the Arrival of the China Dinner Man

PHILIP WHALEN

Did you see that kid from New York
Did you see that invisible flash
Combination cuckoo lemon yard crash
Mumbling all the time. Ring. Send.
Call it so.
The machine can't say any more.

Chez Berrigan, Chicago
1972

Impatient Poetry for Ted and Alice B.

PHILIP WHALEN

Falling down   { Soft
        airplane message: { ear
Fouling up   { exit
Waves on the surface printed on the sand below
Slightly older than God
                       Police and Telephone Business
    return from bath to find my room full of *evzones*
    dancing laughing smoking drinking *ouzo* etc   As I come in
    they flap and scatter towards the ceiling and corners
    of the room. White chickens vanish.
Sleep memory tears Paine
Webber Jackson & Curtis
You can't have one without all the rest
Merrill Lynch
                fall over jump over edge
                 pushed, no difference
                in the middle of the air
                fall intentionally
                    drop
                     ?
She fixed him up with a 300 pound Eskimo
Who kicked the shit out of him
Given a 300 pound Eskimo, what might happen
Give him (or her) back again to Abercrombie Fitch
Return to Sender, never so gently
With love and understanding opened by mistake
Did I fall or was I pushed?

                            April 26, 1972 — May 18, 1972
                            Pullman — San Francisco

23. Drawing by Philip Guston on the birth of Anselm Berrigan, 1972.

From an Interview with George Oppen
and Ted Berrigan

CONDUCTED BY RUTH GRUBER

RUTH GRUBER: Can we talk specifically about your two work, the two of you, your own work . . .

GEORGE OPPEN: I never talk about anything else.

TED BERRIGAN: Neither do I, if you get right down to it! What specific questions will you ask us, Ruth?

RG: . . . I want to know when you first started reading each other's work.

GO & TB: Last week! *(Laughter)*

TB: No, I've read George's work on and off for a number of years, but to tell the truth, it was relatively indistinguishable . . . oh, I'm getting lost in this sentence . . . I couldn't quite distinguish it from . . . I have to say this sentence in some other way. George was one of a number of poets who were being pushed by people I didn't like.

GO: Yeah, well Ted was one of a number of poets being pushed by people that Marvin [Cohen] and I don't like. I ran across his work in magazines, but never really looked at the poems the way they should be.

TB: Whenever I looked at George's works I never saw anything *wrong* with them, but somehow my attention wasn't being gathered enough. Also, I rarely got to see a large selection of work, and for me that's relatively important. Also — I hate to say this in some ways — but with many poets it's important for me to hear them read, and if I can hear them read it makes a lot of difference. However, I did read a lot of George's work when I heard he was going to be here at this conference, and I started noticing certain things about it, namely, how certain words really stood out and sparkled . . . because of the basic almost flatness of the language, so that whenever he wanted a word to really sparkle, it suddenly sparkled. And I started noticing that he is really interested in something that I'm really interested in, which is how you get around the corner of a line; and when I hooked onto that, I started getting caught up in this certain way. And when I heard him read, he read it better than I could have imagined it being read! . . . Then it all fell into place for me really completely.

GO: This is a trouble for us — a lot of people have had this experience hearing me read; it troubles me very, very much. And a poet cannot find out how much of it is on the page and how much of it has to be heard.

MARVIN COHEN: Because you really hope that what's on the page will be sufficient to take care of it all. Because, after all, to hell with tapes . . . it is the printed page that matters, and anybody who writes is bound to be dead pretty soon.

TB: On the other hand, there's another side to that thing, too. I mean, that's all true, but . . . one does like to hear a voice when you're reading, if you can — when you're reading poetry in any case. And you can't, always, because you *can't*, really, it's true — the person is dead, or you never get a chance to hear them read. But if you *can* hear them read, and you can hear the voice — I'm not talking about magic voices, and I'm not talking about a voice like Dylan Thomas's . . . George, I didn't think that you read them right. And I couldn't imagine how they would sound read right until I heard you read them, because my voice, as you can see, is pitched up and forward, and so, that was a difficulty for me . . .

GO: Well, we just have to hope . . . One tries and tries, and sometimes I think we guarantee certain things in the line division — that some words are solid there, no matter how they're said, but you can't quite control the whole reading . . . I know you seem a little more at ease about the business of reading — it's because you're a young fella and intend to go on reading for the next ninety-nine years . . .

TB: *(Laughing)* That's true, yeah . . .

GO: But I can't be doing this!

TB: I'm not so at ease with it, though, but I'm young enough to ride on that nervousness . . .

GO: I can't. We have discussed buying a wheelbarrow and Mary will take me to readings!

TB: You know, there's another thing about your works; it's that in the early sixties in New York, the young guys had Louis Zukofsky jammed down their throats.

GO: Yes, I know.

TB: And I reacted very strongly to that; and I was determined not to like any Zukofsky works unless I really liked them. And at that stage of the game, vast amounts of Zukofsky works were being unearthed and presented—for example, the Catullus works, which I have to say that I do not like one bit, much as I thought it was a great idea, what he was doing with them; but I didn't think they were funny enough . . . because, I mean, it's a funny idea, and I figure if you're going to use a funny idea, it should be funny!

GO: Well, Louis does usually think things are funny in his own way. This is the business of being accepted; there's a gain and there's a loss. When I incredibly got that Pulitzer . . .

TB: Yes, how did you do that?

GO: Lord knows. There were many expressions of surprise. *(Laughter)* A young man—Ross Feld, I think—who ran a magazine called *Ponytail* in Bard College, had been corresponding with great love with me, and so I sent him some works. And among the deluge of letters was one from Ross Feld which said, I don't know if you need *Ponytail* any longer, but *Ponytail* still needs you. *(Laughs)* I wrote back to him, and I said, I will gladly make a compact with you—let us be faithful to each other. *(Laughter)* 'Cause I knew that was going to happen . . . You're saying that about Louis, who—and you should be comforted by this fact—lived through about thirty years of absolute total neglect.

TB: It wasn't that I held anything against him personally; it was that it drew some shade over my eyes to certain other people's works. It was only about two years ago that a friend of mine called my attention to Carl Rakosi's works, which had just been resurrected—actually, it was the poet Bill Berkson, and he had met Carl at Yaddo, and he came and told me that this man was a really terrific man, and his works were really good. And, all by my little self, I had discovered Reznikoff's works, in a bookstore in New York.

GO: That's lovely.

TB: I got it just from the title—the *Waters of Manhattan*—and I said, now this book has to be good. *By the Waters of Manhattan!* And I picked it up, and it was just incredible!

London
May 1973

Destination Moon

for Ted Berrigan

DICK GALLUP

The snow blows in the silence
Like lazy money that
Crosses my eyes
Which try to follow each bill across the street light

All my energy is tied up in couples
Who stroll hand in hand
Through the daily clutter of emotions
Which fall like snow
And cling to things

For instance
I am attached to this chair as it slips away
It has a date with another person
And disappears as my head slowly revolves
To catch your eyes at the corner
Just passing out of sight
Beneath a tattered yellow kite in the air

Over my head in love with this
Tongue-tied as usual
And still a knucklehead in the clutch
My breath escapes me into the cold

Now I've missed you again inside New York City

In lovely winter's white like a distant train
Silence creaks and rumbles
In the space between us are rockets to the moon
Three days past full above the clouds

Goodbye sleet and rain
Green plants on the window sill

Torn socks and ragged shirts
Lay there in lonely bureau drawers
Wait for me to come back
A bit ragged myself
Eyes spinning

Leaving is hard to do
It breaks your heart open
And fills it with oatmeal
Courage to go on is just that
No bull's-eye to aim at
Except your own

Goodbye lovers
Toe stompers
Sweaty dancers
Who gave me ease
And pleased me
And then didn't

Goodbye New York City
Speeding people
Through the Holland Tunnel
Everything is different
Trees grow in the wind
Sweet grasses of the plains
Clarity in the mountains
A red bush in a dark field
Soon I'll hold the syntax in my head
Under a roof with a sky above
Instead of friendly human soot

—Dick Gallup
December 23, 1975

Dream

CLARK COOLIDGE

of being given a book,
out of the hands of Ted & Alice, but somehow
more designated as "Ted's new book," huge, to be
held with both arms outstretched, and all woven
of a material like great colored hemp ropes, the
"title" so somehow inextricably a part of that
weaving that it is now forgotten, and hurrying
to open to the dedication page, for there, and
in each book different, somehow personal to each
person so given, will be a cat for you, a living
cat in a book.

November 10, 1976

24. Clark Coolidge, Ted Berrigan and Alice Notley, 1982. Photo by Ed Foster.

"This picture was taken in Cummington, Massachusetts, 8 August 1981. Elaine and I had gone for a walk in the woods with our kids and Anselm and Edmund Berrigan. Ted and Alice stayed at home with Clark Coolidge and talked, I don't know about what, maybe mushrooms. I took this picture when we got back. Ted said that it was a very serious picture, it showed what they had been up to, "Another Yalta." I think it was the next day that Ted and I decided to be gardeners and go to Archibald MacLeish and ask for a job. That way we could spy on him and find out about Paris in the twenties. We drove over to Conway but couldn't find his home, so we went to a tag sale and Ted bought Alice a present, and we looked at Mina Curtis's house, where Elizabeth Taylor used to live, and drove past the cemetery where a man named Adams, who invented the chiclet, is buried. Also we looked at my birthplace. It was about this time that we went over to the Cummington Community of the Arts and found that they were putting all the books by women in one place and all the books by men in another. Ted didn't think very much of that, but I guess he forgave everyone because he found one of Alice's books very prominently displayed."

— Ed Foster

Providence Going Sketch

CLARK COOLIDGE

In the out-spread plaids of the gravel town-edge,
rod irons and the man walks to his known pickles.
It's a cut where the two roads spring together
and the close of the bay-gash laps outward.
You can't stand up under too many towers, gaunt
lashed-noggin furnace risers ton-prepared for
list and the snail. This is Town Hall Exit
Bartend and the finny-bright wheat-sodders
stand back. It'll be Math here in a minute
of lime-green tines, and the fellow who picked it
knows nothing anymore than munch in the sun.
Potatoes under wickets and the feral drivers.
The railroad is a change-charge of Obsidian
Midnight, locked to the very packet bottom of its
jardiniere whales.
          But here in the drain crease
hillside the finches are sprouting with their
metal spring rain songs. And the drench penciling
down you hear, if not only the hiss high pure pitch
of the inner ear.
          A man with a bundle in his
furbelows hid stops to itch and think and chime in.
By the side by the side where the blinking whistles pass
and the only streamer bound is the frozen.
          General wide
rainlight in the western morning sky, and I dream I
lay hands on the box like torn-ups of the tin on
Monk's roof.

April 9, 1980

Strong Shift

for Ted

CLARK COOLIDGE

I lived in a discouraging startle
but that diminished like never
a freckle
to live dying down the page

These rooms are the mouths of my friends
if not the ears of those
are interminable to me so
I wonder what makes a friend

A pencil is the last laugh
I was told by another, a dead one
who makes some quick days
of my costume a broadcast

I could hire all the members
of my ramble to dissemble
but I can't doubt you

You are my risible
indispensable if not right
short hand
for which there settles no land

June 4, 1981

25. Ted Berrigan and Harris Schiff, St. Mark's Parish Hall, 1981. Photo by Monica Weigel.

Stretching Out in a Regal Bath

HARRIS SCHIFF

you gave me a backache to remember you by
lugging your stupid suitcases half a block
when I could have gotten a cab

Stubborn
that's what you are

I gave you bruises to remember me by
no scars
            but you'll be seeing those marks for a little while

we didn't see a hell of a lot of each other
the last week you were in town
best friends don't have to do that

but I worry
last time I saw you
I hoped you wouldn't die

Don't be dead
I said to you
as you got into your cab

July 1980

To Propitiate the Gods

ANNE WALDMAN & JIM COHN
INTERVIEW TED BERRIGAN

ANNE WALDMAN: Have you talked anywhere about the Berkeley Poetry Conference in 1965?

TED BERRIGAN: I suppose not too much.

AW: Will you talk about that?

TB: In 1965 I was 30, coming on 31, and I'd written what turned out to be my first book. I'd written some of which was to be my second book. I'd written *The Sonnets.* I was ready, in a way. I felt I was a poet and they had this big wingding at Berkeley and all the poets are going to be there and they are all going to give readings. It was this vague, unformulated thing that was going to happen and because I wasn't in on any inner conference I didn't know much about it. I just heard about it. Actually, those guys were to me, guys that were in these books.

AW: You hadn't heard them read before?

TB: Some of them. I had heard Allen, I'd heard Creeley. I don't think I'd heard Dorn or Spicer. I think I'd heard Spicer on tape. Creeley had played me tapes. I had some contacts with those guys. Bob Creeley had me to read at Buffalo.

AW: When was that?

TB: 1964 he had me to read. That was the year I started getting the readings. Steve Katz had me to read at Cornell. I did *The Sonnets* in early 1964, as a mimeographed book, and I sent it to all those poets. Ron [Padgett] and I did them. Ron was the editor of them, in the sense that he published them. It was my press, but he did all the work. He didn't edit them in any way. So we sent them to all the poets and I had responses from some of them: Robert Duncan, Robert Creeley, very nice response from Allen; he'd come to my first reading in New York, which was also in 1964, March. I read at the Metro. Allen had been there, Frank [O'Hara], Michael Goldberg, and people like that. Paul Blackburn I knew, he was a friend. I was picked up on by the Black Mountain poets. The New York guys liked me and all that, but they weren't doing anything except writing wonderful works. They weren't organizational. The Black Mountain poets were still in the thick of the organizational fervor.

Duncan was heavily involved with the organization at Berkeley, as he had been heavily involved with the Donald Allen Anthology. As a matter of fact, Don once told me that Robert had sneaked in about five guys too many into the Donald Allen Anthology.

AW: But it's interesting that in Berkeley, the so-called New York School wasn't represented at all.

TB: But they were invited. But it was the Black Mountain guys that picked up on me. Bob Creeley responded very warmly and Paul Blackburn arranged my first reading. He wasn't at Black Mountain, but he was influenced by that, and of course, Allen, the beats, of which I thought myself one. I thought of myself as a late beatnik, for whatever that was worth. I was pretty influenced by Creeley, although I couldn't see Robert Duncan yet. I admired him as this figure. There'd been this thing at Vancouver the year before, in 1964. I hadn't gone to it, but Clark Coolidge had been there and Carol Bergé was there. Ed Sanders and I had been tapping everybody's telephone and I was hanging around his bookstore. So I get this letter inviting me to come out to Berkeley. I was one of five young poets who were going to read—it was me and Ron. Ron and I were booked as this one item in everybody's mind.

AW: Why, because of your collaborations?

TB: Possibly, or just because of this noise in the air. There used to be these remarks that you couldn't tell our works apart, which was entirely untrue. . . . So I get this letter inviting me to come and Ron was invited too. Ron was in Tulsa—maybe Patty had just had a baby—and I decided I was gonna go. I talked to Ed about it and he was going to go, too. We weren't paid anything—they couldn't pay us anything—but they wanted us to come and they were going to make us stars. They didn't quite say that, but I read it very clearly. They were gonna make us these stars if we were up to it. I was up to it, I thought, so I thought I'd go, and Ed wouldn't miss it either. I hitchhiked out to Berkeley and Ed flew out and arrived the day after I did. And we got there and we went and it was all happening. I went to a class by Ed Dorn in which he talked about famous tombs of poets. I said, "Who's this guy?" And then Ed Sanders showed up, and Gary Snyder. I talked to Gary. Gary came up to me and said I really like what John Ashbery and Kenneth Koch are doing in New York. This was on Telegraph, and he came out of this restaurant and he stopped me on the street, and he introduced himself and I knew who he was and he said, "I like these guys, Ashbery and Koch. I don't understand what they're doing." And I probably said something like, "I'm sure you don't."

AW: Was Gary reading at Berkeley?

TB: I think maybe everybody was going to read, but I don't really know. The only people I know that weren't reading were McClure and Whalen. McClure because he was miffed about something and Philip wouldn't cross the picket line Michael had set up. Gary said to me, "Allen's going to read in two days." Gary said to me, "We're all waiting to see what you can do, boy." I said, "Yeah, ha, ha, ha. I ain't no boy, buddy."

AW: Wasn't it there that Robert Duncan wrote the homage imitation sonnets?

TB: Yeah, but I don't know if they were so much imitations as they were this incredible tour de force. That was at Allen's reading. I got there and I saw Ed Dorn and I talked to Ed Sanders. Jim Brodey was there, and Hannah Weiner. The next night I was there, there was a party at the Wobbly Hall in San Francisco and I went to that. My friend David Bearden was there and another good poet named Richard White, who has since disappeared somewhere. And I went into the party and Allen was there with his incredible white Indian suit on with feathers, his Tonto suit. Who else had a white suit on? I guess Gary had a white Indian outfit on. They looked really funny, like two milkmen. I came in and Allen gave me this big wet kiss and said, "There are thousands of people all around, who would you like to meet? Anybody?" And I said, "Neal [Cassady]. I'd like to meet Neal." So he introduced me to Neal and we became friends. We stayed friends for a couple of years until he died. I saw him in New York a few times. And I met Philip Whalen, and actually, that was the most important meeting for me there. I met Philip and he knew my works well and he knew the magazine. He talked to me about that. I could tell he was this really solid guy who was very friendly and he also had this no-nonsense quality about him. Allen, by that time, felt like an old friend. I mean, he can make himself feel that way to you. Meanwhile, I had this totally competitive eye on Ed Sanders and John Sinclair—he used to come read at the Metro sometimes, and I knew him. I did not know who this Lenore Kandel was, but I figured since she was a girl she couldn't be too good. I mean at that time, it was that way, just to be straight about it. She was just a girl, she wasn't somebody specific. I mean I knew that Diane [di Prima] was pretty good and I had this strange feeling that Joanne must be pretty good, even though I hadn't been able to quite buy it yet.

But Lenore Kandel was just a girl, whereas there were guys who were just guys too.

AW: I was talking to Diane di Prima last week and she said that so many of the talented women of that time and place (New York City or San Francisco in the fifties) who could've blossomed, didn't because they were uninformed. They just weren't getting the information from the so-called master and male poets.

TB: They didn't know how to convert this male information to female value. That's what's different about now. Joanne Kyger had to go around in circles forever. I think Diane stinted on some of her sociological concepts, maybe. But it was true, it wasn't a very good time for women. I didn't know of any young and exciting women poets, and I knew a few who were coming to the Metro, but none of them were very exciting. The most powerful was Diane Wakoski and you could tell that she was going to flat out someplace, she was going to be flat. No matter how good she got, she was going to be flat. She thought that her private psyche was more important than her poems. Kathy Fraser seemed like she might make it, if she could stop being this cornball, or if she could make that into some strength. I think we always thought that if Patty Padgett would be a poet, that she could do it, but she wouldn't do it, not if we were doing it. We thought we knew some terrific women, but they weren't writing poetry. In any case, Allen read. Allen gave a sensational reading and I sat on the stage because it was crowded. The poets were denied seats, but were allowed to sit on the stage and be these stars which for me was great, and which for Robert Duncan might have been a little uncomfortable. He came and sat next to me. I was with this girl. He came and sat between me and the girl. He said, "Let me come between you two." And I said, "Oh, no," and I got up and moved him over and sat back down next to the girl. He was great actually. He knew my poems and by way of showing me he wrote these poems, these sonnets that he wrote while Allen was reading, out of these things Allen was saying and he just showed me this thing on the stage. It was a very magical event. He sort of answered my unspoken comparisons of him and Frank O'Hara, only I didn't have them the way he thought I did. That was in his head . . . . I just wanted to join those guys, I thought they were good poets and I wanted to be one, too.

AW: That's how I felt at Berkeley. It was inspirational as a younger poet.

TB: It was an inspiration, true, but of course, there were funny things going on. Michael McClure was miffed because he thought he should get to teach a workshop and give a lecture and they were only going to have him give a reading, or two or three, whatever, and he thought he was as qualified as anyone else. And Philip thought so too, and Ed Dorn wasn't going to get to be such a big part, but LeRoi [Jones] was. LeRoi couldn't make it because he was just about to go black in this heavy way so he suggested that Ed be his replacement. Now, there was some number to be settled between Charles and Allen, not between them but by the rest of the people, as to which one was really the President of Poetry. Charles took great pains to point out to them all that Allen was, and Allen of course was a little funny about it, in a certain way. All that was going on in a really exciting way. I thought it was really interesting because I thought the Presidents of Poetry were all back in New York, but I actually knew that Allen was the President anyway. You can understand the position I was in. I'm looking at these guys, coming off this nuclear base of John Ashbery and Jimmy Schuyler and Frank O'Hara, and these guys are talking like it's all there. It wasn't all there. However, they had invited both Frank and John Ashbery. Frank was taking an exhibition of Yugoslavian painters, or something like that, around Europe. John was in Europe and they couldn't pay his way back, so neither one of them could come, though they were both invited. I took great pains to find out about that. I was all prepared to let them know that, when they were inviting me, if they thought these guys were the enemy they were letting a wedge in. But they were way ahead of me. There was a really funny scene, like when Allen gave his reading. Robert Creeley said — Allen was pontificating in this certain way — Creeley said, "Allen," right from the stage. Allen was drinking. Someone had given him a bottle of vodka and he was taking a drink and he had said a few things — just Allen Ginsberg things — but he spoke like he really was the President of Poetry, and he was. And Bob said he was a little bit concerned about this public presence that Allen had, and he said, "Allen." And Allen said, "I want to dedicate this first poem to Robert Creeley." And Bob said, "Allen," sitting right there, and Allen stopped and said, "What's the matter, Bob?" And Bob said, "Allen, I'm worried." And Allen said, "Bob, have a drink," just as quick as can be. Bob just grinned and shook his head. The place was jammed with people and Allen gave this gorgeous reading. Neal came before the reading and wished Allen well, and left. The next day, or the day after, Charles gave a big class, not the famous one, but a different one, in which he said a few things about which I was prepared to take issue but I didn't feel it was my time to do that yet. Some funny things about William Carlos Williams. There was some bitchy in-fighting going on there; it was over establishing lineage . . . .

AW: What about your lineage?

TB: I read all of Pound and saw what to put into poems, I got the direct message from Pound—put everything in your poems, everything that's going on in your life, what it says in the letters you get, in the books you read, what you see in the street. I knew "what you see in the street," but mostly to show it all. What you're reading, that it was just as weighty to quote Ron Padgett and Dick Gallup as it was to quote Suetonius or some other Latin poet. I'd taken Latin. I didn't want to put any Latin in my poems, it looked pretentious. I was just happy to put in the quotes by Dick Gallup, so I did all that, but I didn't know how to make it be shapely. I didn't want to make it look like these unyielding cantos, because then they looked like those cantos and they weren't as good. Then I read these poems by John Ashbery, but first I read this book about Marcel Duchamp that Joe Brainard gave me. Joe looked at it and said, "This stuff looks good. What do you think about what it says?" "What it says is great, hope I can fit how it looks into it." We had a totally different approach. It took me a little while to realize that you were supposed to see depth and surface at the same time, because I'd learned everything on the surface first, and from John Ashbery I learned a little bit more about depth. You could force depth on itself and you could make things come out. I didn't want people to come into my poems, but if I could make things come out . . .

JIM COHN: Is that the basic working principle of *The Sonnets*?

TB: Yeah. They're all based on this push/pull idea. Blocks. Blocks is a key word in *The Sonnets*. It talks about blocks all the time and that's exactly what it is.

JC: That interchangeability—I don't know how it related to painting. It feels like an irreverent use of lines and words.

TB: It isn't irreverent either. See, when I looked at these painters and their paintings, I liked them, it was great. I hadn't looked at much painting before, but I wasn't going to put in the colors. I mean, I wasn't going to make abstractions, nor was I going to make representations. I didn't know what I was going to make, but I wasn't about to do any of that stuff because I didn't know enough. Then I read what people said about these people's works and what they said, and I couldn't follow too much of what people said about them, but what they said made a lot of sense to me. Then I took what they said and tried to do that in my poems. Not the way they did it in their paintings, but the way they said what their works were. To me, it translated that they could have been talking about poems, so I tried to do that too. I made blocks of words of four lines, three lines, or six lines and they involved some feelings, simple feelings or complexities of feelings. Well, those were the feelings I was having all the time, mixed with other feelings. I also got totally involved with the sonnet form. I read Shakespeare and I liked it, too. I just thought it was a little neat, but I saw you could make it less neat, you could cut off the edges. Bill Burroughs, John Cage, all that stuff was in the air. I don't know what I thought, I just thought I could do it and then it happened. That's what really happened, and then I did that. Then I got a lot of flak for about ten years for not doing something with that, but I'd already done that, and I didn't want to do anything with it. I only wanted to do it. So then I immediately regressed into writing poems like Frank O'Hara, because he was a good poet who just said, "I do this in my life and I do that in my life." That's what I wanted to do, but I couldn't do it because I didn't know how to write poems. But by doing all that other stuff, I learned how to write poems, and I could do what Frank did; I could write my own poems . . . . [But] I couldn't sustain that line of cohesion and make a good sounding work because I wasn't some Elizabethan walking around flashing images and metaphors. I just couldn't do that. But I could make that structure, I thought. So I did certain imitations, but the only thing that didn't hold up was the cohesion. The idea of the abstract expressionists was, of course, to put how you did your works on the surface, and I decided to do that. I didn't decide so much to do that as see that that's what I would have to do to make works. I understood from Burroughs that you could cut things up, but I didn't want to make these works that looked like they were this one kind of thing, this special kind of information. I didn't want to quite do that. And, of course, poets had been using repetition forever. My favorite poems are full of repetition— "Annabel Lee" and poems like that. The first poem that I understood how it was put together and everything was "The Waste Land," and I think it's very possible that most of my poems that have any kind of craft in them other than the kind that just comes to you sometimes, are probably totally influenced by "The Waste Land." Every bit of other information that I got just served to show me that what I got from "The Waste Land" was true. Of course, I had to get what was in "The Waste Land" without getting that mood, because that wasn't my mood. I was this guy running around New York City ripped out of my mind with excitement.

JC: What did you pick up from O'Hara?

TB: Personal tone. The way to use a casual tone and then long lines without

26. Anne Waldman and Ted Berrigan, The Naropa Institute, Boulder, Colorado, 1976. Photo by Andrea Craig.

having to be measured in a slow way. To write fast. I write fast. I'm fast — write as quick as my hands are. Irish line, he used that. I hadn't seen that being used. It's the way I talk.

JC: What do you mean?

TB: Whatever happened in your life was as interesting as anything else. You come up to your friends on the street and you tell them a really interesting thing happened — I went and bought a newspaper — then what? That was it. And then you say, "Oh, yeah, right. A guy goes and buys a newspaper. Phenomenal." Caesar never did that, couldn't buy a newspaper, didn't know what was going on in the outer provinces. We did everything from the time I came to New York in late 1960 until I wrote *The Sonnets*. We did everything. I remember Dick Gallup and I and Pat Padgett reading in this basement, reading to each other from three different versions of *The Iliad*. What were we doing? Fortunately we were too dumb to be self-conscious about it. At least Dick and I were. Pat, I suspect, was just having as much fun as possible under the circumstances. We thought we were in training to be these great poets, and lo and behold, we were. Ezra Pound said, "Read everything." So we read everything. Then he said, "Study everything." And we said, "We don't want to study everything." And then we found the painters. You don't have to study everything, you just see it. So then we looked at everything up and down Madison Avenue, going into every gallery and looking at millions of paintings. We overloaded the circuits with an unbelievable load of information — and drugs. We took millions of all kinds of drugs. Change your consciousness. I see flat; I take a little acid and I see depth.

JC: What about that persona? That combination of Yeats and W. C. Fields?

TB: That's an afterthought . . . . When I see my poems already written I see they were all written by these personas, but when I was writing them, I wrote that. I don't create a character in the sense of thinking too heavily about it. I just make sure that the character I am creating is a rounded one that has four dimensions. If you're that person, you probably have to be one main one and three shady ones.

JC: Yet essentially, the persona or the speaker is a comic one.

TB: Well, that's Irish, that's the kind of thing I learned from Frank O'Hara, that you had to talk the way you felt. I talk the way I feel most of the time . . . the way the blood feels going around in my veins. I'm an electric wire, not a gas pipe, I suppose, but I had to make it in my poems so that when the "I" is talking, it is not the "I" that's the subject of the verb "think." I think — what do I think? Red Sox — 4, Yankees — 2. I think dark out there, light over there. It's about as far as I go on thinking except when I'm having fun, then I like to think enormous thoughts, structures, palaces, and architecture. I thought plenty about *The Sonnets,* I thought great architecture and rooms and buildings, but I only thought those when I wasn't writing. When I was writing, I thought, "Ah, put these lines in here, write these four lines. What do I say next? Fast." I didn't want to say, "Good." I wanted to say, "Yeah, that works, it enables me to say this." I like to write a few lines and read them in the time it takes me to get the typewriter back over here to type the next line so that I'll know the fifth line comes off the first four and not *just* the one before. But I do want it to come off the one before. I don't want it to come off of something I'm thinking. I can't write any poems in which I detail everything a flower does unless I have a few books around that tell me what a flower does. My poems are like a room, but not this room. There's not enough in this room. This room was made by somebody else. I may live here for three months. I'll make this room look like rooms look.

AW: Rooms you live in? Put everything up on the walls!

TB: Yeah, but it's not even that. It's what's not in the room then, given you have enough time to do it. Plus, the way the towel's on there and not there. What's on this desk. If too much gets on here, I take it away because I may want to write something. If too much is on the floor, I may kick it under this couch because I may want to write something. That's how *I* am. One of my principal desires is to make my poems be like my life, and my life is the way I think I am, because I don't know how I am. I can't see myself the way that you can see me, but I can see everything else around me. If I can make everything around me be the way that it is [in these poems], presumably I can create the shape of the self inside the poem, because there is a person inside almost all of the poems. Sometimes not on stage, but just talking. Sometimes it's the inside of a person talking, but I couldn't have it be inside that person talking unless I created an outside first. Inside doesn't exist without the outside. I want to make the poems have shape, be shapely. I also want to make them have some tactile quality. My technical achievement in *The Sonnets* was to conceive the sonnet as fourteen units of one line each. I don't think it had been done that way much before. I don't think it had been broken down much more than into couplets, so I had a lot more variables to work with and a lot more possibilities of structures. It was just like cubism. I was totally influenced by what my take on cubism was. Take all those planes, put them flat up like this, and they're different. They go this way and then they don't. They turn into optical illusions. They don't go, but you can make them go, you can will them to go, but they don't go just when you look at them. I don't like the kind of reality that when you look at everything, it changes. I like to hold it . . . .

JC: Around the time of your poem "Tambourine Life," were you on the verge of becoming a communist?

TB: I guess that's where I got rid of communism. No, I'm not much of an ideologue. I love to take it all in, but I'm this Irish, Shavian skeptic in the end. That's why I can't quite believe in socialism. I always thought that socialism would be preferable to capitalism. I always despised capitalism as a concept, although I really like the room it gives me. Terrific to be this American. Maybe it would be terrific to be this Russian, too, I don't know . . . . I'm actually a little more warmly disposed towards Buddhism, but in fact, it looks to me that Buddhism would turn into some hideous police-state too, if it were carried far enough. I believe in the separation of church and state. I'm this Roman Catholic, but I don't believe it can work. I don't believe it can work when it's not separated either. In fact, I don't think it can work, but it's necessary. Your religious instincts have to be fed, your religious nature has to be fed and it has to thrive or else you'll just die. There's a big misconception that your spiritual nature and your religious nature are different, but they're not. The need for ritual, the need for order, the need to serve, the need to know you're doing that and to have a community there and be recognized in it is totally necessary. I believe in the ego—it's an Irish trait—and the ego finds it difficult to be subservient to teachers except at a certain distance. My heroes are lesser bodhisattvas like Philip Whalen, Frank O'Hara, Allen Ginsberg. I find those guys to be models for my life. I think it's sad that I can't go to church on Sunday, or whatever day is suitable, because it was a wonderful feeling to do that and believe. I did get to do that and believe when I was young, and now I can't believe that way, though I believe that the people that are doing it are right, as long as they believe that way. And they do believe that way. But that was removed from my life, and it was necessary to remove. I don't, however, feel like I'm in any limbo— I'm this American . . . . I believe in guys that wear coonskin caps and fringe jackets and go traipsing around America—the migrant teacher circuit, just like the frontier scouts. Migrant workers and teachers, I'm part of that. The tattered bodhisattvas who, at best, are fallible, quite fragile too, but incredibly durable.

I can't be the giant organizer, nor do I have too much sympathy for it though I totally admire seeing it in how Charles Olson was, or Allen is. I love to be close to these guys because they give off great darshan and light and energy and generosity and spirit. I love that Allen was always trying to get me to go and meditate, but not heavily, because he wants you to give as much as you can. My affinities are towards the Davy Crockett type . . . . Joe Brainard once said — we were sitting on this bench on Sixth Avenue across from the Folklore Center, Waverly Place and Sixth Avenue — he said, you see these people go by and you realize that they're just in this bubble that they put out from themselves, and that everybody goes around with these bubbles. Perceptive thought. Joe never read any Buddhism in his whole life. It is given to Americans to be naive and underdeveloped and overproductive. I'm all for that. Wisdom now. Hamburger later. Joy now. Wisdom is good; it makes you sad. Wisdom is like LSD. You take LSD and it's a great trip and you feel great and everything looks great but it isn't that way. These colors are going to look like this again when you come off it. Then you look at everybody, at these warm, wonderful feeling people, but you can't touch when you're on LSD — you can only look — and that's extremely sad . . . . God gave us these limited senses because we were supposed to have them.

AW: Do you think we are informing the generations to come just as we were informed?

TB: We only inform them on how to be poets. You can't get a damn bit of information out of the poetry of the past without liking the poetry of the present. Maybe there are a few exceptions. What we do is inform the world now by existing in it, and not by our poems, but by the writing of them. It's necessary for all people to write poems to propitiate the gods. The lack of writing them calls down the mild and modest anger of the gods. That is why we do that, but in order to write poems you have to be a pretty straight-up person and that's only a general statement. Taken too close to its specifics, you don't have to be that, you can be the world's worst person, but that isn't poetry's fault, it's your own. If you are the world's worst person you will either die young or else your poetry will turn horrible. But if you stay at it long enough, all your life, you will be a pretty straight-up person. It is necessary to do that, and we bear witness that it is necessary to do that. That's all. Nothing else.

August 1, 1978

Pinsk After Dark

ALLEN GINSBERG & TED BERRIGAN

Reborn a rabbi in Pinsk, reincarnated backward time
I gasped thru my beard full of mushroom barley soup;
two rough-faced blonde Cossacks, drinking wine,
paid me no heed, not remembering their futures — Verlaine & Rimbaud.

February 12, 1982

Grace

Lita and Morty invited me & Peter
to the Côte Basque, eats 1982,
note accent
William Carlos Williams, help me!
Ezra Pound, don't laugh.

February 12, 1982

27. Allen Ginsberg, Jim Carroll, Ted Berrigan, Henry Pritchett and Louis Cartwright at Allen Ginsberg's farm in Cherry Valley, New York, 1969.

28. Ted Berrigan, Helena Hughes, Allen Ginsberg and (at the door) Jeff Wright, St. Mark's Parish Hall, October 15,1979. Photo by Monica Weigel.

Reds

ALLEN GINSBERG & TED BERRIGAN

There isn't much to say to Marxists in Nicaragua with .45s
afraid of the U.S. Secretary of State, eating celery.
Back in New York, "We saw a beautiful movie," Allen said.
    "It made me cry."
"I hadda loan him my big green handkerchief, so he could blow his nose!"
    Peter Orlovsky laughed.

February 12, 1982

Two Scenes

Time Mag's Central American Expert sd
    Gen. Haig was "an asshole" —
What a surprise in Private on the telephone,
    we dated each other up for next Thursday.

I stood outside the Kiev tonight, nose pressed
    to the plate glass, feet freezing
in city mush, and watched two aging lovers
    inhale their steaming bowls of mushroom barley soup.

February 12, 1982

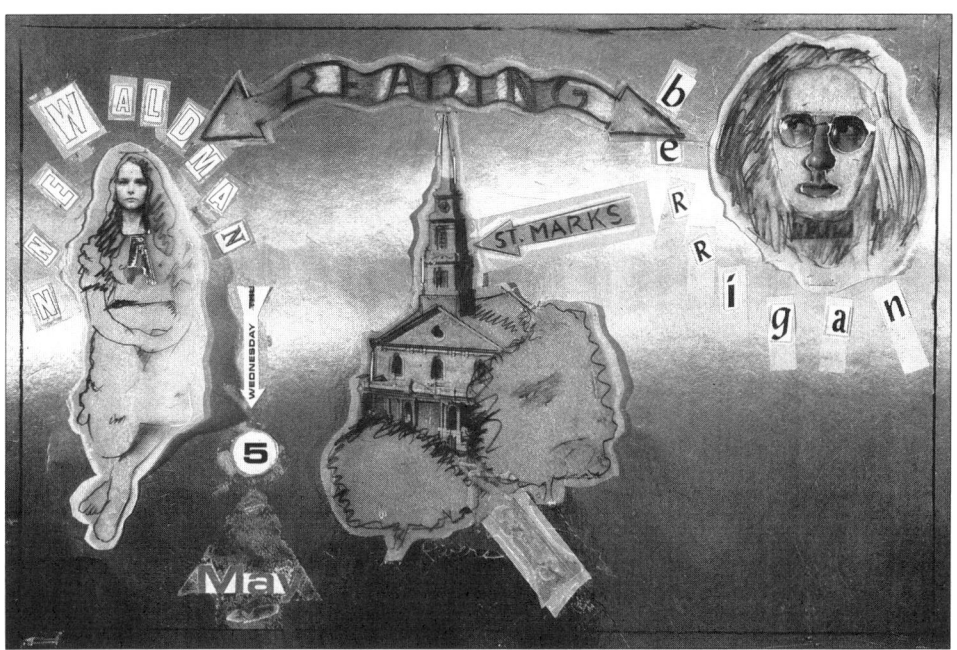

29. Collage by Larry Rivers for a flyer announcing a reading by Anne Waldman and Ted Berrigan, May 5, 1971.

For the Gifts of Ted

ANNE WALDMAN

who wields the press, who takes a
fatherly role, who gets you in his
wicket, who tells you why you might
be sane, who indicates the inning,
who is roomy & ample of dress, who is
wide of thinking, who is, by force of
habit, a talker, who does not wiggle,
whose turf is a shoal, who cohabits with
a gazelle, who is informal in his
shirtsleeves, who is oracular, who
covers his walls with rainbows, who is
pious at times, who is cousin to the
elephant, who is holy of heart, whose

tremors feed the microphone, who speaks
like a volcano, who is a magnetic field,
who is a magnum opus, magniloquent man,
who is definitely not a Mohammedan,
who is friend to the Buddha, who stole
a maidenhead once, who is indomitable,
is indocile, who honors his profession,
who rarely errs, who occasionally
harangues, who has a quick look,
who wears the spectacles of his class,
who devours literature, who eschews the
fairy tale, who is dexterous of head,
who accompanies his friends to the
bookstore, whose tooth is sweet,
who gave up his teeth to heaven,
who is diagnostician of the realm
of the senses, who wears blue, who
carries a bag, who hibernates like the
bear, who was formerly known to dance,
who disobeys but is no anarchist,
whose art is pleasing, who has a
distinctive handwriting, who devises
the donut theory of the universe,
who has no theory, who enthrones
the leaders, whose lack of approval
is a detriment, who laughs the loudest,
who is no stranger to the bed, who
will never be destitute, who coos in
love, who knows the chthonian gods yet
rises up himself to Mt. Olympus, who
forms a cheering section, who inspires
confidence, is a friend to mothers,
whose candor is ruthless, who makes
the arietta sing, who can be a mighty
squall, whose link is to ecstasy.

—Anne Waldman
November 15, 1982

Ted's Old Man

TOM PICKARD

Ted's old man
had trouble with the company
and, as a point of honor
and self-respect, died
when they told him to go.

His old lady applied
to a local party chief
who found her a job
as a cashier
in a school meal's cafeteria.

Ted said come round, Alice is
interested to talk and
can remember folks' histories
a long way back; better
than you could yourself.
It's scary man
when they end up in poems.

Come round. Just shout
up at the window
and I'll throw down
the key.

Homespun

REED BYE

Laughter is the death of time
and time is the laughter of death
Yet death is not a time of laughter.
Does this disprove some Hegelian suppositions
perhaps the very planks of our modern stage?
I rest my case, with one foot on top
waiting for a train
and hear its whistle foreshorten
to higher and higher registers as it nears.
Aha! I think
it would never fall to me
to find pitch a function of frequency
and motion, though voices do get shrill
when they're talking at you.
I turn up my collar and head out of town.
I had hopes too once but they were snuffed
in coffee and sinkers somewhere south of Tri-cities.
I was going to change things too, sure, I know
that's a laugh, hah! That's a good one
Hah hah! Very funny.
But I'm not sad, you see
time changes everything
and though my heart sometimes feels like it's
tacked on the rigging, drying in the salt air, well
inside there's still some thunder now and then.
You see that light up yonder?
There's a kind of a joke.
It's here and then it's gone
but it'll never go out. You ask old Ted,
he's here to tell you.

PART THREE

Last Poem

Before I began life this time
I took a crash course in Counter-Intelligence
Once here I signed in, see name below, and added
Some words remembered from an earlier time,
"The intention of the organism is to survive."
My earliest, & happiest, memories pre-date WW II
They involve a glass slipper & a helpless blue rose
In a slender blue single-rose vase: Mine
Was a story without a plot. The days of my years
Folded into one another, an easy fit, in which
I made money & spent it, learned to dance & forgot, gave
Blood, regained my poise, & verbalized myself a place
In Society. 101 St. Mark's Place, apt. 12A, NYC 10009
New York. Friends appeared & disappeared, or wigged out,
Or stayed; inspiring strangers sadly died; everyone
I ever knew aged tremendously, except me. I remained
Somewhere between 2 and 9 years old. But frequent
Reification of my own experiences delivered to me
Several new vocabularies, I loved that almost most of all.
I once had the honor of meeting Beckett & I dug him.
The pills kept me going, until now. Love, & work,
Were my great happinesses, that other people die the source
Of my great, terrible, & inarticulate one grief. In my time
I grew tall & huge of frame, obviously possessed
Of a disconnected head, I had a perfect heart. The end
Came quickly & completely without pain, one quiet night as I
Was sitting, writing, next to you in bed, words chosen randomly
From a tired brain, it like them, suitable, & fitting.
Let none regret my end who called me friend.

— Ted Berrigan

Written for the Memorial Service

KENNETH KOCH

I admired Ted's stubbornness and single-mindedness and his total dedication to poetry. Our first meeting was when he came to my office at Columbia, in 1962 — Ron Padgett was in one of my classes — to "interview" me, mainly about John Ashbery and Frazer's *Golden Bough*. This first time I saw Ted he was very mild, earnest, serious, and scholarly. Next, Ted and Ron, along with Lorenz Gude, had founded the great *"C"* magazine. He was writing a lot. He and Ron invented the Poetry Machine, which produced poems ad infinitum. I was here and there and from time to time a rumor would reach me of Ted's being a founder and king of the new New York School. I saw this impressive presence, both like and unlike the serious student whom I'd met before, at parties and readings. Hey, Kenneth, I really like what you said to Mike Goldberg, Ted said. Kenneth, where can we read some of your poems? You know down here we don't read *Poetry* magazine.

Ted was, I heard, magnetic, a father, a leader, he held things together. His poems were getting more and more accomplished and beautiful. I knew, for the first time, how good he was when I read "Tambourine Life." I loved (love) that poem. It seemed in a way ahead of everything — absolutely casual, ordinary, and momentary-seeming, without joking, mystery, or false dazzle, and full of buoyancy, sweetness, and high spirits. Ted told me that my poetry had inspired him. He was a generous man. I don't think I ever told him how he influenced me. He did, by that poem maybe most of all — though it was years before I tried anything like it; by his poems in general with their very particular kind of honesty and their being open to everything; and by a letter he wrote me that said something about a poem of mine that not only made me happy but changed a little the way I wrote. I wish I could find it (the letter) — as so much of Ted's well-known daring and original great-good-heartedness. Along with being brilliant (and encouraging) Ted was one of the funniest (wittiest) people I've known.

Poetry, what poets write and how they think about poetry, will be full of Ted for a long time. Life, however, is different, and sadder, and less, without him in it.

St. Mark's Church In-the-Bowery
July 8, 1983

30. Flyer by George Schneeman for a reading by Anselm Hollo and Ted Berrigan, at St. Mark's Church, 1974.

For Ted

ANSELM HOLLO

It is 0200 hrs July 8, 1983
and I am "lost"
for two-three hours
in Man-Eating District

drunk, hot, almost shitting my pants

"Hollo found dead in alley
on eve of Berrigan's funeral"

but "live"
to pity myself some more
and to compose
some regrettably maudlin verse
to recite at the service

5 years later
I don't know what to say
except that I'm trying to be less sloppy

while still munching my daily
ofttimes with dread
in this best-of-all-possible

where sometimes your lines
leap off the page

to make me laugh so hard I almost shit my pants

February 24, 1988

For Ted Berrigan

ROBERT CREELEY

After, size of place
you'd filled
in suddenly emptied
world all too apparent

and as if New England
shrank, grew physically
smaller like Connecticut,
Vermont — all the little

things otherwise unattended
so made real by you,
things to do today,
left empty, waiting

sadly for no one
will come again now.
It's all moved inside,
all that dear world

in mind for forever,
as long as one walks
and talks here,
thinking of you.

Ted

TOM CLARK

Choking on la phlegm fatale
malady of the moralist obsessed
by art-as-words-as-life
Though you outsurvived Kerouac
by several months' tenure
on the planet you died the same death
internal combustion of the blood—
Jack, your great hero (along with Frank)—
whom, in your sole encounter,
you appeased with obetrols,
an interview, and reading of "Tambourine Life."
"Get your teeth fixed," Kerouac told you.
When you departed (you later recalled)
Jack looked sad, because you were
"taking all the energy out of the room"
& that's how we feel now.

★

"Just like the old days, only
we are crazier than ever,
and more parts ache, too!
I have a sore leg, backache,
my radiator's thermostat seems
busted, and my wheels
are less than rims now.
Still, the mail must go
through! But where did all
these fucking Indians come from?"
                              —T.B., letter, 18 Dec. 1981

★

The phone rings & you're dead.
"Put it on the cuff," you used to say, riding by;
"go now, pay later."
Now it's later & the bills are all paid.
You told me many things
useful to the management of heart
& mind
         tho there toward the end
things got too retrospective
to be behavioral; & finally
I got 2 messages from you
out of that period of which
you told Simon Pettet "wearily,"
"last year was the worst."
The second was: "the pentagon
still hates you, but you are
a major in the army of the young,"
& the first was: "dear tommy: love
spurs us on, you & me, to
only one death. that is why
you can just call me 'laura.'"

                 ★

What to do when the day's heavy heart
produces baffling combustions everywhere
southwest lost doubloons rest in memory
& the best of urban voices gone

                              —Tom Clark
                              July 5-8, 1983

31. Ted Berrigan, Jim Brodey and Tom Weatherly at St. Mark's Parish Hall, 1981. Photo by Monica Wiegel.

Because We're Here

For Ted Berrigan

JIM BRODEY

One Star is designated, located just above the moonrise, as Ted's star.
When I talk to Ted, I speak directly to his star.

Looking at your star tonight
Yes that one over the moonrise
Seem to sense you're in town

We don't need no reason

To see you lying on our floor
Your spirit's too heavy to disappear

And we're too drunk to let it
Vanish or let it just go back
Wherever you've been lately

Your star twinking out there
Has a halo of yellow light
So bright as you were

Because we're here
And you're not I sing
To you shining brother

Because we're here
In your great light tonight
I sing rejoycing in your light

Your star rises
In this evening sky
And we are watching

We are remembering
How you were
When you pushed us

Further than we thought
We'd ever go because of you
And your head full of ideas

Because we're here
Is because you're not
And we sing your song

The stars are out
But none are as brilliant
as your own star

Over the moon that's full
I have to laugh
As I cry for you tonight

Shielded by your own light
In this great motion
You wielded w/ poems

Your life and ours
Have never been the same
Your weight of love

Can never be met
W/ anything but
Our finest voices

Because we're here
To witness this night
And the one star

Whose light guides us
In your spirit
Let your music play

Let the poems speak
Give me the power to sing
Oh singing eyes

Oh relentless friend
To all who seek a voice
Your light may heal us

Because we're here
In this bright midnight
Looking at your star tonight

—Jim Brodey
November 27, 1986

32. Ron Padgett and Ted Berrigan reading their poetry at the Kornblee Gallery, circa 1965.

A Personal Memoir

ARAM SAROYAN

I'm not sure when I first met Ted Berrigan, but the first vivid memory I have of him is at the party Frank O'Hara and Joe LeSueur gave in May of 1964 for the Italian poet, Giuseppe Ungaretti, a magnificent white-haired old man. Frank and Joe's loft below Union Square on Broadway was teeming with New York poets that spring afternoon and evening. Along with Frank, there were James Schuyler, John Ashbery, Kenneth Koch, Allen Ginsberg, and LeRoi Jones, all of whom read from their work toward the end of the party. And they were followed by Ungaretti himself, who read with such thunderous passion I found myself moved despite the fact that I knew no Italian. Younger poets, though none read, were also out in force: Ed Sanders, Ron Padgett, Dick Gallup, Tony Towle, David Shapiro, Kathleen Fraser, Jack Marshall and Jim Brodey I remember, and I'm sure there were others. At one point, Ed Sanders circulated a request for a single pubic hair from each poet in attendance. I wasn't certain how to comply, exactly, but Allen Ginsberg standing nearby quietly reached into his pants and extracted the item, enlightening me. The collection — carefully labelled in glassine envelopes — was later offered for sale to literary collectors through Sanders's Peace Eye Bookstore mail-order catalogue.

At that time, Ted Berrigan occupied a position somehow *between* the elder and the younger poets. Only shortly before the party, I had come across a copy of his legal-sized, mimeographed magazine, *"C,"* at the Kornblee Gallery on the Upper East Side, and I was aware of him and his Oklahoma cohorts Ron Padgett and Dick Gallup, as well as the young painter and writer, Joe Brainard, who did the *"C"* magazine covers, as a sort of high-spirited band of young mavericks — though their allegiance was firmly to the New York School (O'Hara, Ashbery, Koch, etc.) — who had come to town and were in the midst of making a splash with their talent, wit, and — not least, so far as their immediate contemporaries were concerned — effrontery. In fact, Ted was older than the others — twenty-nine at the time, the same age as LeRoi Jones (a year or so later, Imamu Amiri Baraka) — but he was the editor of *"C,"* and the group's unofficial mentor, so one tended to think of him among the younger poets. To give a sense of a particular approach he could take socially, I can quote a remark he made to me that afternoon.

First, though, I should say I was a native New Yorker who, at twenty, had just made my official debut as a poet with six poems and a review in *Poetry* magazine. I was terribly serious about poetry and I immediately sensed that my literary "stance," to use a word favored by the group of Black Mountain poets I looked to (Creeley, Olson, Dorn, etc.), wouldn't be much to Ted and his group's liking.

However, when we said hello and someone made reference to my recently published poems, Ted surprised me by responding in a warmly positive tone. He was a bearded bear of a man even then, but at the same time there was something easy-natured and relaxed in his manner that released me from the reticence I might ordinarily have felt.

"But you don't really *like* my poems, do you?" I asked him.

"Oh, man," he answered, in his Oklahoma accent — he was from Providence, Rhode Island, but had gone to the University of Tulsa on the G.I. Bill after Korea — "I think they're elegant. But I wish — I wish you'd tell a few *lies* in your poems. You know?"

I smiled at this, but I *didn't* know. And yet I liked it, somehow, anyway. The Black Mountain style is a valuable, exacting medium for a young poet, but I was apparently ready just then to be given the keys to a more carefree vehicle — if only for an occasional joy-ride. "My friends and I like to tell a few jokes in our poems sometimes," Ted added, "since we *are* real poets, like Frank said in his poem 'Why I Am Not a Painter.' I think you'd be good at that too." In the nicest way imaginable, Ted was telling me I might lighten up.

This was the first of many acts, tactful, sweet-natured and full of a real generosity of spirit, that I was to know him by during the next couple of years. He published my poems in *"C,"* as I published the *C* gang's in the magazine I started that fall, *Lines*. We collaborated several times on poems, writing alternate lines on the typewriter at night in his brightly lit Lower East Side apartment, the walls of which were full of Brainard's intricate, mandala-like collages, as well as works by other painter friends of the New York School. He favorably reviewed a chapbook of poems in which my work appeared with that of two other young poets. We gave a reading together. And he wrote an introduction to my first small collection.

But more than all of that, he let me see his life with his first wife, Sandy, and their two young children, David and Kate, in a way that comprised an implicit acceptance of me as a person — something, I realize now, even more important to me at the time than his literary approval. For all the bluster and bravado he could summon at certain moments, Ted was essentially a shy, deeply caring, most tender-hearted man. This unexpected glimpse of his own deeper self was offered so off-handedly that I only half-consciously recognized the personal generosity implicit in it.

He was, in this way, the least parochial of poets. He was an Irishman from a working-class family in Providence, a Korean veteran who had done his Master's thesis at Tulsa on George Bernard Shaw. I was an Armenian Jewish New Yorker — son of a famous writer — nine years his junior, who would seem to have shared so little of his background and allegiances that all but the most casual friendship would be a virtual impossibility. Yet, somehow, during those first years on my own, Ted was a combination of friend and older brother, critic and collaborator, teacher and general interlocutor that made him perhaps the essential figure of my beginning as writer and adult, equally. And, like his mentor, Frank O'Hara, he assumed at least as large a role in the lives of many others. His presence was like a warming sun at the center of the downtown literary life.

Years later, after getting married, moving to the West Coast, and becoming a family man myself, Ted was still an ideal reader at the back of my mind as I wrote. One of his memorably telling responses to a piece of writing was to mark it — in a soft, erasable pencil — "A + " meaning the writer had given a marvelous performance, maybe just a bit too marvelous to be, after all, anything *more* than a performance. The style and substance of such a criticism was particularly salutary to a young poet in the first, heady flush of his powers. Ted could kid one out of an assumed portentousness faster and more painlessly than anyone else I knew — sometimes merely with laughter.

But as compelling as Ted's presence had been to me, inevitably, over the years of not seeing him, I gradually all but forgot what he had meant to me. Then, this past fall, I called him long-distance about a line from a poem of his I had in mind to use as the epigraph for a piece I was writing. Three thousand miles away in New York City, someone picked up the phone and said hello in a barely audible voice.

"Ted?"

"Yes." The voice was only slightly louder, and not particularly friendly.

"This is Aram Saroyan. I . . ."

"Who the fuck is Aram Saroyan?" he said in a slow grumble, and then I could hear his familiar, soft, bubbling laughter. "How are you, man?" We talked that afternoon for about an hour and I hung up the phone astonished and moved. "Why did you wait so long to call?" he asked at one point in the midst of a mutual torrent of reminiscences. It was a naked, lovely thing to say, even as I felt bad for him saying it. And then, reaching into the mysterious heart of our friendship — we had been discussing, among other things, my book *Last Rites*, about my father, and a lunch the three of us had shared years before in New York — he said, "I'm in this with you for life, Aram."

33. Ron Padgett at the Memorial Service, St. Mark's Parish Hall, July 8, 1983. Photo by Sharon Guynup.

So it is now, having heard of his death at forty-eight on a sweltering July 4th in New York City, I feel even more poignantly what he intimated. He gave me a large permission, both exhilarating and chastening, across the threshold of my chosen path. He let me see him on his own path — as it has turned out, all the way through. The relationship was real, troubling, finite, and beyond any measure I know. He was a great, surprising gift in my life, Ted Berrigan, and I won't be able to forget that again.

— Aram Sarovan
July 1983

34. Kenneth Koch at the Memorial Service at St. Mark's Church, July 8, 1983. Photo by Sharon Guynup.

35. Greg Masters and Michael Scholnick carrying George Schneeman's portrait of Ted Berrigan in a procession following the memorial service. Photo by Sharon Guynup.

Sestina

for Ted

BERNADETTE MAYER

As love as what by chance as brotherly
waits for words to quote brilliantly singly
abstract as an elephant's ivory requiring to talk
to you the lighter lily equalling 1934 or some other
date old. Buried friend you left me through death
else in a life as what as this

radiating world we did lean together in that
outrageous of the sunflower now so fatherly
because lost in the speed of sudden okay death
past of disorder has been finally married
to that least and most desired other
in a stream of the pardoned partner talk

of something or the spotted touch-me-not to talk
with you was often to listen to the rosy this
rock hardy enough to take it or else
be your identity, a man so sisterly
hell's angel's ardent fingers themselves so bigamous
a number on each hand, now part memory

remind me of our teeth and the tooth of memory's death
or the Chesterfields of a daddy as who talked
and talked they flee from me & everyone is gay
who sometime did me seek & there were all those
drugs, now not so, you should've been more motherly
towards yourself and kinds of others

Husbanding immortal time of poetry and other
matters till much later than it did death
the old aunt of the sisters would come like a lover
without emergency (this world), with secret talking
whispered & bruited about now shouted by all those
people living in our community

You trickily left us staggering like a moth o friend
while you got to die and be the desirous other
of a matter changed apart from a word yet these
anywhere words laugh & don't with you on death
needing the garden of talk and noise, to talk
with another to live and be alive as a lover

Goodbye ally outrageous relation
moth of suffered pleasures talks now with another
community, answers death just with poetry or else.

— Bernadette Meyer

7/4/83

CAROL GALLUP

A note marked, not for reinvestment.
Total loss, of punctuation,
walls, don't you want to reject your nails,
where did I put what I was thinking of?

Years ago, I dreamed he died of his sins.
It was a Catholic dream with "of his sins" in it.
Sitting down to a meal when we heard the news,
I began to cry into my salad.

Just friends, what else? all those times
(include the ones I've forgotten) (most of them)
add everything that happened that year.
Beginning, middle, end, & all gone,
gilt picture frame laid squarely over corpse
(showed those lines to Ted).

Marlon Brando as husband drops his hand
open, palm up, on sofa, movie wife
rests hers in it, Ted admires this
"Roman gesture," details he finds or thinks up
the classic "oh really, how would you like
a punch in the nose" (cheerfully,
put to a 3rd person)

Why don't you be your share,
fat Irishman? Not the one
who lives upstairs, but the one
upstairs in the Horrible Galanthea,
1962. Young together, add sex & pills,
it will be necessary to scatter the chickens.
We were to invent the Marx Brothers.

For 21 years, consciously inhabiting the same planet.

36. *Face of the Poet*, by Alex Katz, 1977. Oil on aluminum.

Remembrance of Things Fast

MICHAEL BROWNSTEIN

I remember meeting Ted for the first time at the corner of Sixth Avenue and Eighth Street in December 1965. From 1965 to 1969 and 1970 we saw a lot of each other. I miss the sixties precisely in the way and to the extent that I miss the image of Ted in the sixties; I can see him clearly, standing on the sidewalk outside Gem Spa at 4:30 in the morning, talking a mile a minute about everything in creation until the veins are standing out in his forehead, his face covered with sweat, a ragged tan corduroy car coat pulled up around his ears against the wind, his eyes laughing and also glittering like stars. In those years we walked all over the city at all hours of the day and night. Ted walked faster than anybody else around then. He was fast and sharp and clean. I remember once in the summer of 1967 when Anne and Lewis had left their apartment on St. Mark's Place for a trip to the country, and Ted had the keys, and we stayed up all night writing a sixty-page letter to Anne and Lewis and the universe. When I rang the bell that night, Ted opened the door revved up and completely naked, and I'll never forget his trim hips and haunches; his flat stomach I can see clearly, as if it were yesterday.

And he won't call me up in the middle of the night a week after we first met, waking me up to invite me down to his apartment and watch while he rearranged the paintings on the walls. We won't ever shoot speed again together, that's for sure; I got sick for six months while Ted just slept for two days, he must have been stronger than me after all. I won't get to have him explain to me exactly who the good and bad poets were, who was faking it and who was stale, who still had a chance and who shouldn't even bother. He won't grimace and roll his eyes anymore whenever I use words like "epitome" or "incisive." He won't turn on all the lights upon entering a room and explain how bright light was important, and then ask me if I have any Dave van Ronk records ("You smoke too much pot, man; all you have here is this head music.") He'll never tell me again, "You may see me take drugs, but I'll never smoke cigarettes or drink." He won't ask me each time he sees me if I have any new ideas. He won't tell me to meet him at Brigid Polk's room in the Hotel George Washington at 2:00 A.M. and then not show up, leaving me alone with a supersonic lady who wants to make rubbings of my penis. He won't tell me about "presence," about how it's the only form of Oriental religion he needs. He won't tell me not to call him Berrigan, "My name's Ted." When he took me to a party at Kenward Elmslie's house on Cornelia Street in 1966, I felt too abashed to say a word, I didn't know any of these elegant people he introduced me to. "Well, there's hope for American poetry yet," he said, when after numerous excuses I finally got up the nerve to go out on the floor and dance.

— Michael Brownstein

Strange To Be Gone in a Minute

STEPHEN RODEFER

At any rate Ted Berrigan will be remembered by those who knew him, and did not, for what he did and more importantly what he wrote and conceived of doing.

Once at a party at the Berkeley Poetry Conference in 1965 (at Dave Haselwood's I think) it seemed both wonderful and astonishing that he accepted without a blink a copy of Frank O'Hara's *Lunch Poems*, only just published, handed wryly across a circle of hands and glasses with the bright request, from Victor Coleman, would Ted sign it. And unflinchingly, immediately, he did, much obliged. No one quite could take it in, but that was part of it. It was a very terrific and funny moment, prolonged. So the movement carried you on, laughing, looking for the upstairs.

And a few years later when "Tambourine Life" hit the stands, it really did seem that one of the major drafts always in the offing had arrived. The freedom-of-information act you could never rescind, from one of the best minds of the *next* generation, with the chops to fix it up again.

And every time I open *Many Happy Returns* or *Nothing for You* (Ted Berrigan's titles were always careful and brilliant, without seeming to be either) I'm astonished by what fine love poems are there. Read again, for instance, "Words for Love," the first poem in *Many Happy Returns*.

So what, if sometimes he was rather bent or blue or out or off, or even at times was an absolute terrorist of dyspeptic opinion and self-indulgence. It would be stupid and self-righteous to criticize the year or condition in which his life ended as intentional or unconscious suicide, or as a forewarned move on literary history. He did what he did, and there was no gain without say — for he was amused and alive; and all those vital or fatal humors were intelligent to a disarming degree, even when you didn't get it. You might have been delighted, if you hadn't been so stupified. And to be incensed was really too bad, or just dumb, the next day, after he had gone.

The year before last, at a Langton Street residency in San Francisco, how he groused or pricked the vauntingly guarded crowd ("80 Language Street" as Michael Palmer was calling it). But who could discount an evening of Berrigan's inimical blitzkrieg discourse, always more thought-out than you thought — "I am a national treasure" — especially when it was followed by a reading of *all The Sonnets* straight through! It *was* an historic event, even when you thought such things were no longer possible. And it was a *national* (certainly) and absolutely as well (who could not hear?) *treasure* of a work. The deep-flung hook had snagged a big one, and most people in the audience had known it from the word go. The mad, gay, young Manhattan just before it flopped. But the mind had struck, with the prepossessing attention to take art and life to be matters of pleasure, not judgement.

Once recently in San Francisco, after having called Bob Harris's dentist for something or other, Berrigan asked whoever was driving to pull over and he'd run into that bar to take a leak. Ten minutes later (we were late), the motor running, getting in, Ted recounts something the bartender has said. Then after a pause, scratching his left elbow, adds that he always took it to be honorable to buy a beer after using an establishment's john. It was part of the virtue a person should maintain on entering any premises.

Just yesterday I bought *So Going Around Cities* in Lenox, Mass., signed "Ted Berrigan — on the premises." And so he was, and will be I imagine for a long time, just as he deserved.

— Stephen Rodefer
July 10, 1983

37. Miniature oil painting by Ann Mikolowski.

38. Miniature oil painting by Ann Mikolowski.

Things To Do
After a Nuclear Disaster

KEN MIKOLOWSKI

say hello to Ted

Call Me Berrigan

Persephone said, I never met him. Yes you did, Lani said, he was a big man, big head of hair, big beard, great big belly out in front of him — he was bigger than his body, actually.

Dear Pat:

I was sad to have to give you the news about Ted, but then I know I have been bracing myself for the news ever since sometime in 1976 when I was in Montana. I pulled my pickup over beside the Yellowstone River and wrote an elegy for Ted one day. I was in tears because I was sure that Ted had just died. The cosmic grapevine had told me. Luckily I was prudent enough to file the poem and when I got back to Berkeley, I asked around and found out that Ted was fine. This elegy I will have to dig out and use; of course, I may not use it. Bill Berkson said that they didn't know what exactly Ted died of, but I think the right question is *what didn't he die of?* and then go get some.

Actually I may write an elegy for Ted, but only use the dedications that he scrawled in my copies of his books while he was waiting for me to finish cutting up the cocaine. I said, while you're waiting — sign all your books for me so I can sell them after you're dead. "Sure," Ted said. And he did cheerfully, because he knew he was about to get high enough to enjoy himself for a few hours. And Ted also loved the truth.

> for Keith Abbott
> the most
> lily-white
> innocent soul
> West of the Mississippi,
> from his slave,
> Ted Berrigan
> June 24th, 1981

I wasn't the one in my family who first met Ted. When Lani traveled to England, she asked me if there was anyone whom she should look up. "Ted Berrigan's in England," I said. "I've never met him. Why don't you look him up?" Ted, who believed in the diplomatic system, approved of this. I believe he preferred young poets to send their wives to him, to break the ice, so to speak.

148 / NICE TO SEE YOU

In fact, he used to tell the story of how Lani appeared in her snow white outfit on the University lawns to rescue Ted from dreary students who were quizzing him on *his methods*. Lani remembers it differently. She said that she went to the Berrigan's apartment. Alice, who was pregnant, let her in. Ted was upstairs. "Alice," he was whining, "come upstairs and fuck me!" Lani introduced herself to Alice. "Alice," Ted continued to yell, "come upstairs and fuck me." Alice yelled back that Keith Abbott's wife Lani was here. Silence. Then Ted said, "Did she bring anything?" "Yes, two bottles of Guinness," Alice said. "Well, send her up!" Ted yelled. Lani said that Ted was called Edmund at his pub. Whenever the woman at the bar saw him come in, she set up a bottle of tequila. "Edmund!" she'd say. She had to order it special just for him, no one else in the town drank tequila.

      for Keith,
    ⅗ of my
  best book of
    all
       time,
  love,
    Ted Berrigan

That was written in my copy of *In the Early Morning Rain,* a book that I bought in Carmel, California. That book was a miracle that saved me from my in-laws, who were visiting us in Monterey. They were nervous with nothing to buy, only the beach and the ocean and the bay. Before they came to pick us up and take us to Carmel, they bought a TV set and stand from the motel they were staying in. They were nervous in our front room without a TV set in it. Anyway, they were delighted with Carmel because there were lots of things to buy. While they were doing that I wandered into a chi-chi greeting card shop and there it was! a big blue book with yellow and white covers. Berrigan's new book! I didn't know him at the time but I loved his sonnets. So I took the book to a city park and it saved the day. I didn't think it was a very good book, unfortunately, and said so in a review of Ted's work. Ted, of course, had a memory of an elephant about reviews of his own work, and remembered it some eight years later when he was writing his dedication: "⅗ of my best book." Actually I think he's still being generous about that book; two fifths maybe.

```
        for Keith,
            from
        his student,
            with severe
                respect & love,
        Ted  Berrigan
```

When Kenward Elmslie came to the West Coast, he asked that I read with him at the Poetry Center. I doubt that I would have ever read there otherwise, and I appreciated the gesture. However, Ted came into town and needed money, so he was shoehorned onto the bill with us. We read at twelve noon. Ted and I made it, but neither of us were steady. Twelve noon after a night of fun, that old imaginary c&w tune was our theme song. Luckily, Kenward was terrific and he sang and carried on. Ted and I repaired to a bar afterwards. We sat there with our drinks, quiet, and then Ted said, "I want a Collected Ted Berrigan next, right after Frank's, just like his. I don't want to die but I do want that book. Actually, I don't mind dying but I don't want to be carried to the hospital all black and blue, that's for sure."

```
        for Keith,
            The Mayor of
            Casterbridge from
                his friend,
            Ted Berrigan
        The Rector of Justin
```

When I came to Chicago to read at Ted's course, I brought along some pills that I had been given. Ted traded me some red and black capsules. "You can probably take these," he said. "You're *younger* than I am." I asked him what was in them. "Well," he said, "the individual who sold them to me said that if I couldn't handle them, he would take them back." Ted paused, and looked out the window at the gangs cruising the opposite side of the street. "But he was arrested that night for beating up some old woman in her house." I took the pills with me to North Carolina but I didn't try them. Two days later at the airport, I was waiting for my flight to Arkansas and I felt tired and so I spilled out a little on my finger and licked it. I had a lecture to give that night and I needed some help. I was sweating bullets twenty minutes later, and when my flight changed into a prop plane and began picking up crippled Vietnamese refugees, I ordered a double Jack Daniels. I barely had it in my hand before the stewardess came by. "You'll have to finish that now or give it to me, we're about to land, sir." *But we just took off,* I said through clenched teeth. "Sorry," she said, holding out her hand, "regulations." I drank the double and got off the plane in Fayetteville shaking and sweating and dragging my left leg — which seemed to be permanently asleep. The last time I saw those pills was when I gave them to Andrei Codrescu at a Joanne Kyger reading. Twenty minutes later he came back and began jerking at my arm. "That was acid," he hissed at me, "not speed, *Assid! Assid!"* When I lodged a protest with Ted some months later, he laughed. "I didn't say they were good, I only said they were strong," he said.

(In his book *Nothing for You*)

> Remembering all the Nookie
> we've shared
> For Keith, from Ted,
> *Take this title literally.*

Ted had wonderful manners, and he was consistently kind and generous with me. He still always reminded me of a grade school pal, someone who talked loud and took up space and had a comeback for every remark, however crude. In our last correspondence I received a series of postcards with childish crossouts and messages such as "Dear Keith, everyone hates you in Bisbee! Love, Lou Costello." He also sent pasted pictures of animals with "the new york school" scrawled across the bottom and signed "by Clifford Styll" (sic). In a trash job for an old school teacher I came across a child's bulletin board paste-up of famous American authors. The student had used Author cards, framing them in construction paper and writing underneath them, "James Fenimore Cooper, his novels showed a sense of the Western Frontier, etc." I got a publicity photo of Ted from Blue Wind Press, cut it to fit and pasted it to the display with his name under it and then mailed it to Ted with the caption, "His poems showed that he owed Keith Abbott $25 for some speed."

> for Keith,
> Cole Younger's
> no. 1 Mojo,
> from
> The Sleeper,
> Ted Sleeper

In Chicago Ted and I went down to the local bar on his block. It was a grimy workingman's bar. I only wanted a six-pack of beer to go, but once Ted got there, he had to sit for a while and catch his breath. "Ted!" a voice said. I turned and saw a pie-eyed crazy moving in on us. He had a stained grey overcoat with a knife slash between the first two buttons. He was smiling, but it was a terrible smile full of busted teeth. "TED," he said, fumbling in his pockets, "TED, uh . . . ." Then he *smiled,* thinking about what he was going to say. "TED," he said, "here's that money I owe you." He handed Ted some disgusting dollar bills. "Thanks," Ted said. He pocketed the bills. The geek wandered off. Ted and I sat there for a moment. Ted said, "The first night I came here to this bar, that guy came up to me and asked me for some money. I had some, so I gave him a couple of dollars. Turns out he is the bar creep and I broke some terrible rule by giving him money, but ever since when he sees me, he remembers and he pays me back. I'm the only one that ever loaned him any money and he keeps on paying me back." Ted laughed. "I'm *making* money on this deal." When we went back to his flat, he smoked a little of the new California sinsemilla I had brought. It took him by surprise and he sat in his chair by the window for two hours without saying anything. Then, he noticed me coming out of his study. "I'm tired of being the Dashiell Hammett of American Poetry," he announced. "From now on, nothing but big dense poems. Actually, I've already been writing them, but I didn't know what I was doing until just now." I was impressed by the way that Ted taught his classes in Chicago. He let his students come over to his house and watch him do what a poet does. I remember the apartment house there when I first entered it. There had been a birthday party and the only thing in the house to eat or drink was a pair of Jim Beam pints. Some students were in Ted's workroom, looking over his journals. Ted got out of his chair and walked past. "Look at that," he said, pointing to one dark page. "We wrote that one night in blood. We were shooting up speed and we thought that our blood looked terrific!" He laughed. "Look at it now, ugh! It looks *horrible!*" My Irish responded to that in Ted, the sense of how awful things sometimes turned out and yet, hey, that's a *different* kind of awful, isn't it? To quote someone on a New York painter (and which was used for O'Hara in turn): "He was always out here, buying a piece of the environment." The word environment doesn't sound right, but that's what Ted did. He seldom got more than pieces, but that's the way things went with Ted. Sometimes they were big pieces, and he was consistently considerate and daring and yet tough with them. He was always there when he had to be.

Many Happy Returns
    Darrell Gray
       Feb 69
   formerly star
       student of
          mine
    at the U. of Iowa
  sold this
       out of starvation &
   despair, and
        it was happily then
bought by its
          only
       truly discerning
  male reader,
    Keith Abbott,
  who is adored by
    Ted Berrigan

Good-bye, Ted, thanks
    for the memories
we
    remember you well,
who call you
    friend,
       Keith

               —Keith Abbott

Writing Against the Body

DEATH IN THE AFTERNOON
She sighed in vain for the chaff and
the wheat, not knowing
the one from the other.

CHARLES   BERNSTEIN

Contradictory impulses characterize my approach to Ted Berrigan's work. It seems easy to become caught up in the circumstances and style of his life, to portray the man in terms of his personality, his influence, his often extravagant behavior. Such a perspective, however, whether the response is positive or negative, not only deters attention from Berrigan's writing but also tends to misconstrue the nature of his significance. For Berrigan's work—less interrupted than completed by his recent death at forty-eight—can most usefully be read not as a document of a life in writing but, inversely, as an *appropriation* of a life *by* writing.

This inversion of conventional "confessional" style is a key to Berrigan's method. Inversion is both a formal and a moral technique for Berrigan, which partly accounts for the anxiety generated by his flips of self and text—text overwhelms self, self overwhelms text. Many of Berrigan's admirers and detractors share a misconception that his work is an extension of diaristic "self" writing, despite his decisive break with such practices. What makes Berrigan's writing difficult to understand—or deceptively simple—is that he built his edifice on the wreck of the old—using its broken shards to build a structure with altogether different architectural principles.

The Sonnets—with its permutational use of the same phrases in different sequences and its inclusion of external or found language—stands as an explicit rejection of the psychological "I" as the locus of the poem's meaning. This rejection, however, is complicated by the enormous pull *The Sonnets* exerts on readers to project onto the text a cohering "self" even in the face of overtly incommensurable evidence. (Transference may be a more apt term for this than projection.) This is an enmeshment that not only the reader but the author may fall under the sway of. Indeed, Berrigan has (as in different ways much current poetry has) mined this misprisioning for its considerable emotional power—tail spinning self-implosions and self-explosions with remarkable dexterity on the principle that such power is too much to give up, because, quite rightly, a writer can't afford to give *anything* up.

                                        Frequent
    Reification of my own experiences delivered to me
    Several new vocabularies

One of the risks of this enterprise is that the detritus of this project-in-
writing — by which I mean "the lifestyle of the poet" — now as ever runs the risk
of being taken as its flesh.

                          The poem up on the page
    will not kneel   for everything comes to it
    gratuitously

The biographist fallacy substitutes the chaff for the wheat by renormalizing
this *body of work* into a work of "self." In this way, the production of meaning is
trivialized as personal gestures rather than *read* as inscription in a text.

    I'm only pronouns, & I'm all of them, & I didn't ask
        for this
    You did.

So there is nothing *simple* about the biographicity of this work. For any
self-celebration there is also self-destruction, in the sense that for Berrigan the
morning — meaning dawning — of the self is also the mourning — meaning
dissolution — of the self. The fusing of form and subject matter is evident: the
"integrity" of the poem/body is "violated" by various literary or corporeal
"abuses." Note that the body is an overt metaphor for a coherent, integral,
individuated self — it gives a biologic legitimacy to the concept. Berrigan's
work is, then, a sustained assault on the sanitized body of the "self" (*health*) and
simultaneously on the sanitized body of conventional verse (especially the
furnished souls of confessionalism). In this textual practice, health is both a
grammatical and a psychic fallacy. Health suggests an "objective" criteria for a
normalcy that, in Berrigan's terms, would be the death of the psyche, which is
to say the death of the body. To write outside the sanctioned subjects and
syntaxes of health is to be forced into a situation of desperation: to be able to
continue that work may require the sacrifice of, at times, more than can be
sanely or gracefully accommodated into a life. Berrigan's writing poses the
startling fact of writing's lethal and consuming importance in requiring the
yielding of body and mind to its inexorable priority. It's always hard to
understand how writing can *cost* so much — because it seems after all just putting
words on a page. Berrigan's power was to incorporate that cost — of the
creation of a psychic space in which writing can occur — into his texts. Writing
against the body he was able to realize an image of it.

We are drawn to shit because we are imperfect in our uses
of the good.

I was charging others to love me, instead
of doing so myself.

You shout very loudly.

break yr legs & break yr heart

We ate lunch, remember?, and I paid thé check

The pills aren't working.

Such an urgent approach to writing needs to be situated not in a personalist interpretation of the man but rather in the context of the national and international sociopolitical climate of the early 1960s, during which Berrigan's formative work was written. That is, it is important to understand this work as originating in the period prior to the widespread and highly publicized political and cultural oppositions of the late 1960s and early 1970s. America in that slightly earlier moment was infected with an unspoken violence, a violence masked by anesthetizing/neutralizing/nullifying forces marching under such banners as nuclear security, counterinsurgency, American will, falling dominoes, cold war conformism, preparedness, suburban comfort, self-reliance, and self-actualization, etc. This dizzying succession of rationalizations demanded more that the lip-service opposition of a writing that was otherwise content to go about business as usual. However, Berrigan's commitment to writing "over and against"—that the body might be destroyed in order for its truth to be told—did not preclude comedy. The humor in this work is related, in part, to a disequilibrium of scale—the (f)utility of individual rejectionism against the backdrop of Multinational Steel and Glass, circa 1961—as if meaning could be produced by sheer force of will, charging at windmills. The problem is that this work has a wake often more visible than itself that blends with the historical—you might call it psychological—that such work does not come cheaply, can be no kept avocation, but must be torn from—*out of*—life.

Morning
          (ripped out of my mind again!)

The biographist fallacy misses the boat for the water by focusing on the tactics that have allowed for such writing. These tactics are no more than the exigencies of being able to go on with the work; though it bears saying that such tactics — desperate in the logic of their pragmatism — need less to be judged in the abstract and more to be understood in the context of the necessity of continuing without the luxury of second-guessing the means by which this is made possible. Though we all can and do second-guess others and ourselves daily with paralyzing monotony.

> I have had the courage to look backward
> it was like polio
> I shot my mouth off

It is a measure of Berrigan's times and not only of his life that such a project-for-writing took on these particular necessities. There are, of course, other quite different courses — but none less radical, none less serious about the production of writing — would seem to justify that journey.

> The only travelled sea
> that I still dream of
> is a cold, black pond, where once
> on a fragrant evening fraught with sadness
> I launched a boat frail as a butterfly

— Charles Bernstein

Written on the occasion of a memorial reading for Ted Berrigan at St. Mark's Church, November 15, 1983. Epigraph and extracts are from *So Going Around Cities* (Blue Wind Press), Berrigan's Selected Poems. The final quotation is Berrigan's working of Rimbaud.

39. Anselm, Ted, Edmund and Alice at 101 St. Mark's Place, New York City, 1982. Photo by Sheree Levin.

Invitations/Visitations

TOM SAVAGE

I knew Ted Berrigan for about seven years. Learning from him as a poet and a teacher was the most important part of that experience, but what he taught about how to act as a human being toward other human beings made him, at least in our small community, one of the most outstanding practitioners of the Buddhist principle called "metta" (universal loving kindness). He did not practice Buddhist meditation of any sort. He simply embodied this principle and called it "heart." Shortly before he died, he took pleasure in having been told by a doctor that he had a "perfect heart."

He saved my life twice. For some years I lived in a Long Island City standing-room-only hotel. As a young bisexual man who had just come out, I was making all the mistakes I should have made in my teens. I had antagonized the members of a neighborhood gang who threatened to murder me. When I told Ted about this, he initiated a grant mechanism that got me the money to move to Manhattan. Two months later, the tenement I'd moved into on East 7th Street burned down. Ted went over to the fire to try to help me get my stuff out and later put me up for a night in his apartment.

For a number of years I wandered around, psychologically shell-shocked by these and other occurrences. During this time, Ted made himself available to me as adviser, father-figure, confidant and fear-shrinker. Alice, Ted, Anselm and Edmund often seemed to be the only real friends I had. What patience Ted had, that allowed him to listen to my problems, day after day, sometimes for hours at a time! (Sigmund Freud gave Mahler six-hour sessions but Mahler wasn't very often in Vienna. I was always in New York and within easy walking distance of the Berrigan-Notley flat on St. Mark's Place. But then Ted had a perfect heart, unlike Sigmund and his followers who may have a gift for empathy on demand but who are mostly interested in making a living.) Ted was the first poet to extend me an invitation into his home after my culture-shock re-entry into America at Naropa in 1975 after four years in India. It was several invitations and about six months before I visited him the first time. I hope he never regretted inviting me. He would have had to have been a saint not to regret it sometimes. In April 1983, he was kind enough to invite me to read with him at St. Clement's Church. Sadly, it was his last full-length reading. I feel honored that we read together and grateful that he helped me to dismantle the watercloset of despair into which I'd fallen.

Six years ago, he gave me a cat who still punctures the hours when my solitude turns into staring-at-the-wall loneliness. Her name is Hetu, which is a Pali word meaning, roughly, "cause and effect."

— Tom Savage

Sonnet for Ted Berrigan

HELEN LUSTER

Grey his head goes his feet green.
Sonnet #47, one of Ted's.
I have to make sense and be literal. He
has no such limitations. Now. Or then.
I'm Dragon Lady, she who slithers. Yet must wait
for free-fall-phone-calls. She has balls
bouncing off her head on the Naxco plains.
The lines are for a purpose. Where are the Crystal
Entities? Their wicker wallpaper left behind.
I'm on my way except for banana curves
and toaster reflections. Oh yes, ferns out on the balcony
across the yard, from Robert Graves.
I wish for a clincher line about the Pleiades.
I have Omni. Entropy cancelled before Christmas!
A Remembrance of Ted Berrigan

A Remembrance of Ted Berrigan

MICHAEL SCHOLNICK

Then, in springtime of 1976 the first time I saw him: With a few companions, Ted leisurely strode east on 10th Street alongside the ground of the St. Mark's Church In-the-Bowery. And he paused to show these friends something, or to insist, or to reflect. The sun blared in each charged atom. He'd come to New York from Chicago and lived at 101 St. Mark's Place. That summer I went out to Naropa Institute, while seventy-five people attended Ted's workshop at the church. Sanguine, he there mentioned that in terms of exact dates he stood closest to Amiri Baraka and Peter Orlovsky. This casual observation represented a hallmark of Ted's personality. He could put seemingly inconsequential data into a unique and illuminating context. His poems too, combined with an inventive wit, are rooted in everyday matters.

I finally heard Ted hold forth in a classroom setting when he taught another summer workshop for the Poetry Project in 1978. Always provocative and serious, he offered that his genius included the ability to improve nearly any poem submitted, such was the technical expertise he would impart. Also, it often occurred to him, while contemplating a word in a poem he was writing, to substitute opposites in an effort to complete the poem.

"Most poets are experts in paying infinite attention to their own speech," he said. "One must likewise be cognizant and heed the language which reels about everywhere else." Another disarming piece of advice Ted administered to us one evening was never to cease creatively writing, manipulating words, making poems. Let a few idle days slip by perhaps, but you might become rusty in a matter of weeks.

That same summer Ted read in a new series at the El Centro Bar. He wore a brand-new wide-brimmed cowboy hat to that event. God, when he delivered "Autumn's Day" I pined for grief although, actually, a torrent of happiness surged through me.

Ted's health worsened in 1981. Bedridden three weeks due to complex back pains, he was admitted to Bellevue Hospital after X-rays revealed a kidney stone. A patient directly to Ted's left, a black man, lay with all ten fingers amputated, the victim of frost-bite. Ted supplied him with a Sunday newspaper. To himself he prescribed narcotic mixtures and the nurses obliged with the needles. During my visit he read aloud "The By-Laws" and "Me & My Enemy (All Alone & Feeling Blue)."

A few months later, he and Alice and I discussed Paul Mariani's biography of William Carlos Williams. I said, "There's no reality in Williams's poetry." Ted's eyes brightened. "That's very true," he admitted. "And yours is a statement that only we can understand, this afternoon, now, while I finish getting dressed and put on my pants." He and I then walked down Avenue A. An old, old man passed us carrying a bag of groceries. Ted also witnessed the agonized steps, the pale white skin, the near-fanatical determination. Even so, he questioned me. "Why didn't you aid that old man, Michael?" Ted wanted to turn back the clock, all the clocks, leap over the hedges and chain-link fence of the Village View Apartments, run, tuck a baseball mitt under his arm and refuse the elderly person's gratuity after performing the service.

I once told Ted, "I think 'People Who Died' is an excellent work." He pondered this judgment for a moment and said, calmly addressing Alice, "I think I got, hit, every word right in that one."

Friends were drawn to Ted's fearless nature. Strangers, too — breakfasting adjacent at Dojo's, say — rejoiced in his generous temperament as I mingled with his ineffable endurance. Other poets were especially rewarded by his unremitting praise and by compliments that one could sink one's teeth into. He called an art review I published in the *Poetry Project Newsletter* "a thing of state" which is the type of golden nugget he proffered with the utmost respect and conviction. For love, I was presented with a collage by Joe Brainard, a sobering, remarkably tactile work, executed in collaboration with Ted in the early 1960s. In March of 1983 I spent my last intimate hours with Ted. We dined and partied at the invitation of poet Jeff Wright and family. Ted had just completed on tape a scholarly and no doubt ardent interview with James Schuyler and, unrestrained, he proclaimed this fact joyously. Everyone's buoyant sense of pleasure was apparent. Our diverse conversations beforehand concerning work, marriage, and social news centered at table on an exchange of religious views and notions. In the hazy, high period which followed, prompted by Alice, Ted merrily retold, with amazing detail, the story of one night in Tulsa, Oklahoma, starring his colleague, Ron Padgett. It seems that Ron, on the eve of his departure for college in the east, had acted rather out of character under the influence of a new drug. Ted mimicked the poet's mother — "Ronnie, Ronnie," — and father — "Ron, what did you take?" — as they queried silent Ron who rested in bed, fully clothed, covers drawn up, a few thousand dollars tucked away in his boots. Ted and Dick Gallup, of course, were loose somewhere in the sinister dark. Ted had a ruthless and affectionate sense of humor and he regaled us with this anecdote.

A few minutes later my wife Nellie and I struck a deal with Ted, trading some of our marijuana for several green and white capsules. He and I went along bounding from the doorway, east a few paces, north one block on First Avenue, quickly down 12th Street. It was raining and a harsh wind was blowing. Neither element fazed Ted. I fled upstairs and back with the pot. In the hallway, standing by the foot of the staircase, we saw John Godfrey entering the building. "The red ghost," Ted joked, referring to John's sweater.

Over the ensuing weekend, Nellie encountered Ted on the corner of 12th Street and First Avenue. "Hi, Ted. I didn't see you at first." "I was thinking," responded Ted. "When I'm thinking, I become invisible." They stopped into the bodega and Ted bought a Pepsi. Nellie, delighted by the episode, remarked how tiny the seven-ounce bottle looked in Ted's large hand.

In May on a warm afternoon I spotted Ted and Steve Carey on St. Mark's Place. What a sight, yes. Motionless faces, staring straight ahead, relaxed, they walked in a certain unison, not at all content. Life is hard, Ted would've explained. He believed in aesthetic perfection and in magic that transcended the odds. He was persistently knowledgeable. His commitment to the crafts, both of writing and teaching, was devotional and pervasive. As he wrote, he will never go away. His proud poetry makes me glad.

— Michael Scholnick

40. Steve Carey and Ted Berrigan in front of 101 St.Mark's Place, New York City, 1979. Photo by Monica Weigel.

Walking with Ted

BOB ROSENTHAL

Ted had a big stride. He walked and stood confidently on the sidewalk, at the
curb, or in the street. Walking with Ted, I had to look up to him. His dark hair
shot back off his face and dived down the back of his head. He had a full head
on me. Reaching with each stride yet engrossed in the moment the words the
eyeballs. Sometimes with a few dollars, Steve Carey and I will go to Mac-
Donalds and buy cheeseburgers and walk up First Avenue feeling like kings!
He didn't look down while he talked or walked. One could take in a whole
dilemma and the avenue. If I sit long enough at Dojo's on a nice afternoon,
somebody I haven't seen in five years will come by; that could be good for ten
dollars. Just like, uh did you see that guy? Yeah. Just checking. Or on the day
my back went out, I was in pain and on muscle relaxers, we were most likely
walking to see Joe at the check cashing place on Fifth Street. I swallowed a
painful spasm and a deep rrrrrr came out of me that Ted noticed. Is that you?
That's very becoming.

January 1984

Ted Dancing

BOB ROSENTHAL

He was a middle swinging, foot hopping dancer. He liked to move in and out of the music. He danced quietly while playing pool. He stood up for Irish music. Ewan MacColl or the Clancy Brothers. Like half the world, the Rolling Stones at parties. Livingroom reverie eyes closed, neck loose, dancing from the knees up. Ashes scatter. Bobby Dylan, Eric Anderson, Dave van Ronk. All of his music in words. "You dance just like me you just jump up and down!" Jimmy Rodgers, Sonny Terry and Brownie McGhee. I think Ted danced before or while he read "Yellow Man" at Charas. He was extremely funny. Ted offered me a chance to read in his living room in Chicago. I read about an all night party, 1969, Iowa City, which the cops tried to bust up by cutting the electric juice to the Mother Blues. Everyone snake-danced and beat cans for hours. Ted came up after the reading and said, "Man, I was at that party!" Dancing madly with one girl and then jumping onto another girl on the floor. Beautiful body statement enacting the five fights Ted never had. "At the Electric Circus, the Velvet Underground was playing and there was a totally great light show. I snuck up the back stairs and found Andy bending over the light show. He looked up at me and put his finger to his lips."

1984

(Untitled)

GEORGE SCHNEEMAN

He was a lousy
poker player
Raised too much
Talked, didn't
know the value
of the hands.
He was too busy
with the faces
at the table
to remember
his hole cards.
He drew out
four fives
on Ron
the last time
I saw him play
He was lucky. He had
no business in the hand.
I thought we'd make
some easy bucks
off him when he got
his big grant.
But I guess he
knew his limits
because he never
played again.

41. Birth announcement by George Schneeman, 1972.

Our Love

EILEEN MYLES

No, it's not about greatness
or being human—lucky or
unlucky enough to
hear bombs falling
outside your window on
the Fourth of July, 1983.
Some people have stayed
up, some voices are out there
talking, jawing through
the night and across
the stars I'd like
to connect a couple
of humans and I do
so silently I introduce
them like children
do—they assume
that all the humans
they've ever cared
about should meet
and will somewhere
in time and the
summation of all
those meetings
somewhere tell us
that we have a function
just to be alive and
hope. The tone that
they call elegiac
doesn't do justice
to anything at all
this one night
you may be missing
and I am even
beginning to resent

the light accompanying
me since the world
seems a little thin
or smooth without you. It's
alright to pick
up the phone
and it's pretty late
like someone sleeping
whole needs to
know what's missing.
The details escape
me. Someone who
knows wants to know
more and they
couldn't know enough
I couldn't tell
them that the night
is so elegant
and life seems so
much deeper just
for a moment in
your vanishment
you almost exposed
its secret.

—Eileen Myles

Miserable Life

STEVE LEVINE

To climb the stairs with
    slippers,
To slip off with every step.
    To feel
One's foot slipping, or to
    not to.
To put one's foot, then,
    (An
Accident) into the one
    wet mud
Rut (and splatter the one
    woman you
Love). And at the theater
    to shove to
Slip in, just to sit behind
    a Giant.
And, also, at the moment
    your most
Grandiose train of thought
    is pulling
Out, to know your close
    friend
Is dead; and then, again,
    to go on.
Ted, in the dead of winter,
    to spread cold
Butter on soft bread, to go on
    to eat one's
Daily tiny eggs in order . . .
    Then, when one
Must fish life's wet bar of soap
    out from under
Some furniture, to find it covered
    with horrific hair

Of cat, fur, and feathers. To do
   this. To do
That. To do this. To do that.
   This is not at
All amusing! Miserable Life!

                              —Steve Levine

Hey Ted

MAUREEN OWEN & SANDY BERRIGAN

Tall dark handsome
You are not
in front of Gem Spa in muggy summer   or
"in bed with a crab"
always having the right 34 thousand words
for any given moment
you came into this world smelling like a rose
with a Pepsi in each fist waving waves
graciously   inflicting   "Shaktipat"
from the air & writing about your red
nose so we all thought tho yours actually wasn't
who were you, Ted, then
Who are you, Ted, now?
What was it you said . . . . "A man's love is
like a radiant horseturd" . . . ?
I was a sucker in your radiant arms
"Oh, help me if you can"
How do you feel now?
that morning of your wake I looked at
the azurity of the sky & thought in
Spanish ¡Ted no va a ver este dia!
¡O mi corazon!
¡Recuerde!   Remember!
Let me speak,
Talk about you. A word
in edgewise   what is more brutal more
difficult than the world going on . . . as though . . .
as you'd say
imagine something more weird than having someone's
ear bitten off in your mouth
walk in and have heart failure
You gave everything else you had
Away. All Over This Land
"Words for Love"

Too many little flowers wilting in summer heat
Groan.   You
a little boy   "I picked my first one
read it aged three."
I cried in a cool bar   I cried in a blue
lake I cried into a sock!   I who once shoved
you into a door jamb furious   wept into anklets! You
would never have believed it.
Who will carry my desk to the roof
Praise my pants off   or
not Let's face it you made the phrase
"Bicycle Irish"   a reality to us all   friends
crawled home from you never wanting to hear the
sound of the human voice again   only
to return the next day
with Pepsis, pills, books, peers, cats, dogs
You locked the door, pulled down the blinds
pulled out the plug.
In a blue bath towel at parties
that crested at dawn stoned & speaking &
living everywhere   streets were softer then
tempers kinder   we were all one large nobody!
We were like young lawnmowers!

—July 15, 1983

Notes to "Hey Ted":

"Tall dark handsome" refers to "Feminine marvelous and tough."

"in bed with a crab" is from *In a Blue River*.

Pepsi: Ted's drink.

"Shaktipat": instant illuminating enlightenment experienced at the Guru's.

"A man's love is like a radiant horseturd" refers to Ted's poem "Cowboy Song."

"that morning of your wake" recalls the day of Ted's funeral.

"I picked my first one read it aged three" plays off Ted talking about having read 30 books by the time he was three.

"Words for Love" is a poem title from *Many Happy Returns*.

"Bicycle Irish" is from an old Irish joke. It's someone Irish who talks so endlessly you get a tired ass from sitting there listening. (Also implied is the realization that the speaker even when repetitive and boring is somehow fascinating enough to hold your attention.)

The Rare Birds

for Ted Berrigan

AMIRI BARAKA

    brook no obscurity, merely plunging deeper
for light. Hear them, watch the blurred windows tail
the woman alone turning and listening to another time
when music brushed against her ankles and held a low light
near the table's edge. These birds, like Yard and
Bean, or Langston grinning at you. Can't remember the shadow
pulled tight around the door, music about to enter. We hum
to anticipate, more history, every day. These birds, angular
like sculpture. Brancusian, and yet, more tangible like Jake's
colored colorful colorado colormore colorcolor, ahhh, it's about
these birds and their grimaces. Jake's colors, and lines. You
remember the eyes of that guy Pablo, and his perfect trace of
life's austere overflowings.

                 Williams writes to us
of the smallness of this American century, that it splinters into worlds it
cannot live in. And having given birth to the mystery
splits unfolds like gold shattered in daylight's beautiful hurricane.
(praying Sambos blown apart) out of which a rainbow of anything you need.
I heard these guys. These lovely ladies, on the road to Timbuctoo
waiting for Tu Fu to register on the Richter scale. It was called
Impressions, and it was a message, from like a very rare bird.

To the Muse

for Ted Berrigan
(written at his home on
Saint Mark's Place)

ELIO SCHNEEMAN

I do not always know how to approach you,
You who are never near. I miss your voice
That is air on the telephone.
I look for you in churches, paintings,
In forests where birds fly.
I need you to get me into the sky.
Though you're angry with me,
I'm always around if you want to visit.
We'll make each room our own,
Where I'll exhale fresh flowers,
Because of you.

Half of It

FRANCO BELTRAMETTI

Ted Berrigan wrote a list poem called
People who died
Now he has died too
There is no way around it
Outside it is raining
I remember Ugetsu Monogatari
About traveling in time and space
The pilot a ghost princess
A Japanese movie
Today it is full moon
I just finished glancing thru
Vargas, a Swedish magazine,
Where Ben Vautier says
REGARDEZ AILLEURS!
I already said: outside it is raining
But I haven't said: it is past midnight
Now I said it
I can hear my son now seventeen
Breathing in his sleep
A while ago he was
improving his reading
On the Italian comic *Diabolik*
Then he practiced his
electric guitar
I wonder what and how
are doing so and so
Sure I'd love to love her
and I do
I wonder if next year
I should keep a journal
I haven't done that for years
84 sounds good for it
8 is the ∞ *INFINITE* standing
And 4 after all is half of it
Good night Mr. Brian Eno
KING'S LEAD HAT

Memoir: Encouragement and Variation

VINCENT KATZ

The two most important things I got from Ted were encouragement and the variation.

The variation is where you take a theme from your own or someone else's work or speech and use it differently in two or more poems. For instance, you could start two very different poems with the same, borrowed, line. You might think, if you borrowed a line from a song or from a letter someone sent you, that you could only use it once. Ted showed that you could use it once, then if you wanted a different tone starting with that same line, you could use it again. Ted was a master of the variation. He created, as opposed to wrote, many of his poems. That is, he constructed many poems from pieces of writing or speech he found. But they always ended up his own. And they usually ended up as lovely poems too. Occasionally, you ran the risk of losing Ted in these poems. Too many "lines" and not enough Ted. Usually, though, he'd save it by inserting an outrageous, original line in his inimitable, hilarious sense of humor.

Ted showed how you could develop on the possibilities of a theme. Many writers have borrowed lines. Ted didn't borrow them—he made them his. He took them out for breakfast, lunch and dinner, and afterwards for drinks in a bar. He made them sleep with him, and live with him, and they still do.

Encouragement is when I'm reading at one of those huge St. Mark's New Year's Benefit readings with hundreds of people in the audience. The five readers before me seem interminable, I'm so damn nervous. Finally, Bob Rosenthal is blurting something out about The Throbbers, and I step up, Allen Ginsberg smiling and saying "Have a ball" as I trip lightly up. So I read this poem about Edwin Denby with tons of sentiment and emotion in it. I was sure it was the right thing to do, but it was a little weird in those days of "blue window flux towards minute" poetry. Then, in a natural speaking voice, but somehow resonating across that whole auditorium, I hear Ted say, "Right on, Vinny." He said it so calmly, but I heard it, and he knew I heard it. I stood there a moment shivering, then I walked off the stage.

Thanks, Ted.

Trippin' with Ted

EDWARD DORN

The usage of Ted Berrigan's I have always enjoyed the most was "works" (after the apparatus of intravenous injections) applying to verse work (or perhaps verse werk). We talked of this, and more — with Ted everything was interesting, everything was conversable — last time we were alone together, on a train trip to New York from Baltimore, where we had read for Anselm Hollo's series at the University of Maryland.

We were remembering that old chestnut passage in *Look Homeward, Angel* about the train race to N.Y., where the engineers, firemen, passengers and porters on each train got into it with bets and cheering. Ted suddenly whispered, Damn, and took his teeth out of his mouth — "these things just get in the way."

I can't think of a single poet I have known, read or read about in the 20th century who combined intelligence, literacy, wit, naturally accumulated knowledge, and breadth of human outlook, with the felicity of Ted Berrigan.

His "failing" was that his subject matter was limited too often to his friends, or circle. But that limitation was also his humility, possibly his greatest strength. And that is a quality so alien to the modern mentality in any line of work as to make him what he surely never wanted to be — unique.

April 19, 1987

All in All

JEFF WRIGHT

Ted tells Steve Carey and me a peyote story. About seeing his body on the bed, but he was by the window. The feeling of schizophrenia. Another story about Ron Padgett cooking first egg—breaking it and saying, "Zen (!)" Sound of egg hissing in pan.

Steve and I start to tell Daddy stories and Ted picks up the phone.

Originally they'd been talking about Lord Buckley—prototype beat slang king hipster and after they did many imitations of, "Here come de Naz" and "What's de matter wid you baby?" and "What you want, babes?" we went on to all the Zen books we'd read and then to a moment, Ted said, when he realized he knew everything he'd ever know. And I added, but it seemed I had to relearn it all all the time, and they agreed to that.

March 10, 1981

Slaughter of the Waking Arms

STEVE CAREY

Briefly . . .

Culprit finale

River logic

It is a song of usual
    and triumphant nature

It is a fine song

Passing strange

Passing fine

Highfalutin [highfaluting]

Asprawl

The quibbling wrist of spite
    or:
Spite's quibbling wrist

Tag: Berrigan put it best
or:
He put it best

So if you're so's to be
    up and around
      as my mother used to say

Title: Prime Time

The massive assembly
    of the heart

Flabbergasted palaver
    —remember dream of
      trying to remember—Ted

Chatter master—Ted

Palaver master—Ted

Master, lastly, to palaver — Ted

Hatless — Ted

Office [of] [in] repose — Ted

He never lost his life — Ted

Terrible to suppose

Luster sun [sun-luster]

[A] single chime

Fantastic plea

[The] trembling proximity

Title: Archival Stills

Title: Slaughter of the Waking Arms

Title: Adornment of the Rose

Break the narrative

Raggedy shave

The promotion of
        silence & understanding

A flicker

All to [for] long-winded haiku
        raise your hand

What manner [of] craft
            or:
What manner transport

Brackets of life [and living]

And some verb idiot cent

Maya death

Some fatal Sally
        [knew something of flight]

Is it purity or gain
        drives men to flight?

I can live [now] with the adjective

Extended grammar

Plurality divine

Consultation vs. impulse
        [aged]

Smile at the crooked line
        I remember

Hello [ancient] handwriting

I need the narrative

Just as good as I'm
As I'm

Title: Say Nothing

"I quit"—a workshop

Not all things
        are for the scanner

Five in

Take a might line
        [against the twit]

Advertised as amber [beer]

Connote the vowels

Tributary storm
        of ferment

[Some] life-changing line
        of intent

"Are you sure?"

—Steve Carey

Calm Under Fire

JIM CARROLL

We die in different directions
At the same pace we die
As the virtue of structure and grace

As a challenge to distance
We die, you and I, with our hands
Outreached, by chance, one night each
Toward the other. In a corner.
In a cellar. With jars and webs,
A continent apart, we die

As submission to an unfinished heart

1983

42. "Berrigan" — Cartoon by Dave Morice. Words by Ted Berrigan.

I Loved Ted Berrigan

JOHN GODFREY

I loved Ted Berrigan in quite a few ways. I like to think he appreciated that I gave priority to his writing and his sense of art in poetry. He came along at a time when it was important to American poetry for a remarkably fine artist to come up from his kind of working-class, ethnic background. When I consider his roots and formal education, it's astounding that he was so fine an artist. He became one of the elite without any kind of head start, and it will always inspire me that his works transcend his tools. His sophistication in his works is never effete, which is one of the most wonderful standards of the art any poet has ever given me.

Personally, I loved him for his compassion, which could surprise me on occasion even after I got used to it, because otherwise he gave the impression of fierceness and opinionation. He liked to arrive at judgments, and when he did so his liberality and sympathy were conspicuous. He liked to tell me who I really was, often just to piss me off. Even then, however much I might object to his take, it was always flattering that he gave me a full-bodied picture of myself. God, how I miss the kind of noisy, contentious, "professional," literary conversation we often had, full of fine points—he was a wonderful causist— and vulgarisms, not to mention vulgarities. Since his death, which I don't so much dwell on as dwell with, I realize that he left me with an enormous vacuum in my loyalties. I knew for years, even though we were never cronies or pals, that he commanded a lot of loyalty from me, but nonetheless I'm surprised at how much loyalty I actually felt for him.

There was a little episode that we remembered emblematically, so to speak, when I'd be at this place and we'd be good and ripped. When I hitched back to NYC from SF in October 1969 I stopped at Ann Arbor for a couple of days. One afternoon we walked out to Donald Hall's house. I don't think we saw Mr. Hall, but on the way back, in the middle of the wide concrete street in that booshie U-town neighborhood, we came across four fifteen-year-old kids with a football. Ted decided we should take them on. On the first play he heaved a high, not too wobbly bomb. I, Frye boots and all, got by all three of the defenders covering me, made quite an armslength catch, and waltzed past two driveways to score. Ted strode down the middle of the street, joined me, and we tossed the kids back their ball. Then we resumed walking back to town, as if that had been all we'd come out for.

Third Pepsi Right Hand

JOHN GODFREY

He says "What's the matter with
going away with no word of farewell?
I could have loved you better but
I wanted you to float awhile in the yellow neon
You watched me walk to the corner
me walk to the corner known by
me as Gem Spa me as Gem Spa"

I lay my shoulder between closed
lilies of day and the scalding spigot
that helplessly and hopefully turned
in his hand from across avenues
His eyes became the newest particles
of songs so old they would never groan

Ghosts and history are in the telling
smell and shininess of their cool skins
Dateline the Elysian Fen Ted's screwgie
a small round ball of smoke issues
from his lips in another tabloid
Fade out radio waves good-bye
Our future now takes care of itself itself
when we assemble in the darkened stadium
Our minds, which are not one, and
our hearts, which are not one, have learned
from him too much the vital habit
"That's grand," he says, " a *hundred* grand!"

Étude for Ten Thumbs

TED BERRIGAN & GREG MASTERS

43. Collaborative postcard poem by Ted Berrigan and Greg Masters, 1982. For Ann and Ken Mikolowski's Alternative Press series.

Duologue for Ted

JOE LESUEUR

(JOE *is seated at his typewriter, staring hopelessly into space, when* FRANK *enters from outside and crosses immediately to the refrigerator, where he takes out an ice tray.* JOE *looks over at him, not the least bit surprised to see him*)

JOE: Oh hi, Frank.

FRANK: Trying to write something?

JOE: Yeah—a piece about you and Ted Berrigan.

FRANK: Me and Ted?

JOE: (*Nods*) About how he became enamored of your work, looked you up when he came to New York, and whatever else occurs to me. I'm having a hard time getting started. (FRANK *begins making a drink*)

FRANK: Why don't you start at the beginning?

JOE: With the letter he wrote you? (FRANK *nods, and* JOE *looks doubtful*) I don't know. I've been writing soaps so long I think I've forgotten how to write anything but dialogue.

FRANK: If that's your problem, write the piece in dialogue form.

JOE: Like it's a play?

FRANK: Why not? Do you want a drink?

JOE: Not right now, thanks.

FRANK: Begin with what we've been saying to each other and then segue into the business about the letter, and go on from there. You can call it "Duologue for Ted."

JOE: That sounds good. (*Begins typing as* FRANK *sits down with his drink*)

FRANK: Try to make it something Ted would have liked.

JOE: Right. (*Types for awhile longer, then turns to* FRANK) You want to tell me what you remember about the first letter?

FRANK: Well, let's see. I called you at home from the museum as soon as I got it. I remember that. You were on unemployment at the time.

44. Ted Berrigan at 630 East 9th Street, circa 1963. Photo by Lorenz Gude.

JOE: That would have been in the fall of '61. I was trying to write another play.

FRANK: Ah yes, following the success of *Cool Wind Over the Living*.

JOE: Very funny.

FRANK: Come on, Joe. You always had a sense of humor about it. Remember how you couldn't find a review in the *Daily News* the next day and I scanned the paper and said, "There it is," and pointed to a tiny headline that read, "Degrading Drama," and you broke out laughing—? After that, you seemed to want the rest of the reviews to be just as bad.

JOE: And they were. But aren't we getting off the subject?

FRANK: Ted's letter, you mean.

JOE: On the other hand, if I'm going to write something he would have liked, maybe I shouldn't worry about it being relevant. You know why I say that? Because I never knew anyone who liked to gossip and shoot the shit more than Ted. So maybe that's what we should do.

FRANK: As long as we talk about something he would have found amusing.

JOE: Or if we talk about you. (FRANK *looks puzzled*) That's something you wouldn't know about. It began after I left 791 Broadway and moved to Second Avenue, and then you had that insane accident in Fire Island Pines—

FRANK: I wasn't around anymore, in other words.

JOE: Right. And that's when Ted became the greatest champion of your work, the leading O'Hara freak.

FRANK: O'Hara freak?

JOE: Sort of like a Jesus freak.

FRANK: You've got to be kidding.

JOE: I'm exaggerating slightly. Anyway, the O'Hara freaks was what I started calling all these young poets who were so crazy about your poetry and influenced by it. And Ted, I could see, really had you on the brain. He could quote you like scripture.

FRANK: You saw a lot of him after you moved to Second Avenue?

JOE: On the street, mostly; I used to run into him all the time. Like the Gem Spa, he seemed to be a permanent fixture in the neighborhood. I could count on running into him at least once a week. It would be late in the afternoon when I saw him, never in the morning, and usually he'd be on the west side of Second Avenue near St. Mark's Place.

FRANK: Doing what?

JOE: Just taking a walk, I think, and hoping to run into someone he knew.

FRANK: And you were out shopping?

JOE: Or on my way home from an errand uptown.

FRANK: How do you know Ted wasn't out shopping?

JOE: For the simple reason that I never saw him with a bag of groceries. I really think he was looking for conversation. One thing for sure, he was never in a rush. But then, neither was I; when I ran into Ted, I somehow always had time for him. We didn't just pause a moment to exchange pleasantries the way most neighborhood friends do who run into each other all the time. I mean, we'd come to a dead stop and stand and talk for as long as thirty minutes about anything that came to mind, one subject leading to another. And at some point, your name would come up.

FRANK: Ted would bring it up?

JOE: As I said before, he had you on the brain. (*Smiles*) I just thought of something. The last time I had him over to my place was for drinks before a performance of some of your plays at La Mama. There's something very appropriate about that. He came with Alice, his second wife—a terrific poet. Damn, I wish I'd thought sometime to ask him about the letter. Maybe he would have remembered what he wrote.

FRANK: I remember that it was a very nice letter.

JOE: That's all you remember? It *was* your first fan letter.

FRANK: Maybe it's in my papers somewhere. Ask Maureen, why don't you? (*Finishes his drink and rises*) Are you ready for a drink now?

JOE: Please. (FRANK *begins making two drinks as* JOE *looks off*) I'd sure like to know what Ted thought of us when he first came around.

FRANK: How do you mean?

JOE: Well, since he wrote to you at the Museum of Modern Art, he must have thought you were pretty fancy. (FRANK *shrugs*) Don't you think he was surprised when he saw how we lived?

FRANK: He didn't seem to be.

JOE: Or our being gay—I wonder what he thought about that.

FRANK: He didn't seem to think anything about that, either.

JOE: Well, it's certainly doubtful that he thought of you as— (*Picks up a book, opens to a marker inside and reads*) "part of the high-powered New York City homosexual scene in the arts and, as far as art was related to money, certain aspects of flashy jet-set society."

FRANK: Huh? What's that you're reading from?

JOE: Roi's autobiography that came out a couple of months ago. That part was about you.

FRANK: Roi thought I was part of a gay scene that had to do with power and money?

JOE: That's what he's written. It would have been more like it if he'd said you were a faggot who was part of a high-powered heterosexual scene.

FRANK: But if that were the case, why would I have been living with you in that dump on East Ninth Street?

JOE: Good question. And he describes me as your shy but likable roommate, with quotes around "roommate."

FRANK: I don't know about your being shy, but I can understand his putting quotes around "roommate."

JOE: It was gratuitous, Frank.

FRANK: Ted thought we were lovers, too, didn't he? He told Joe Brainard we were, and that kept Joe from going to bed with you until I finally made it clear to him that we weren't, and you scored.

JOE: But Roi knew better, you know he did.

FRANK: (*Smiles indulgently*) Anything else you found offensive or inaccurate?

JOE: Yeah. (*Picks up the book*) After going on about how you introduced him to the world of camp —

FRANK: That was probably true.

JOE: — he describes me as someone who looked like "a blond movie star —"

FRANK: What's wrong with that?

JOE : —"of the ingenue type?!" (FRANK *laughs*) It's not funny, Frank. Years from now, people will read that and think I was a big swish. That's how they get everything wrong later, because things like that get into print. (*Calms down as he takes a sip of his drink*) He was at Ted's funeral.

FRANK: Did you get to talk to him?

JOE: Yes, I did. Like me and a lot of people, he couldn't get into the service it was so crowded, and we had a nice talk. He was as sweet as he always was.

FRANK: Then there you are. (JOE *looks at him a moment*)

JOE: I should be more like you, Frank — generous and understanding . . .

FRANK: What?

JOE: No, I mean it. You should have heard the way Ted used to talk about you. He really admired you, he wanted to be like you. And you know how he turned out? He grew a beard, put on a lot of weight, really wasted himself — and yet somehow he looked great, a little like Whitman, and he became a sort of guru in the neighborhood. Which reminds me, the St. Mark's poetry scene is terribly straight. Everybody's married and they all have families. It's a very wholesome scene.

FRANK: That's nice. (JOE *looks off*) What are you thinking now?

JOE: That it's funny Ted never hit the sack with you. After all, so many of the other younger poets did.

FRANK: It's been exaggerated how many straights went to bed with me.

JOE: Has it?

FRANK: Let's get back to Ted's letter. He wrote it from Tulsa —

JOE: Hey, this may not interest you, but Ted sure would've gotten off on it. He loved it when I camped or talked about gay things. And you know why? As contradictory as it sounds, it was because he was so straight; I don't think he had a gay bone in his body.

FRANK: You don't mean he was like Terry Southern?

JOE: Exactly. He thought being queer was a gas, the funniest thing in the world. He really liked it when I carried on. (FRANK *smiles as he takes this in*)

JOE: What?

FRANK: I liked Ted very much, as you know, but at times, I felt there was a distance between us.

JOE: I think I understand what that was from what Ron Padgett said to me once — something about his, Ron's, having such respect for you that he tended to be a little formal with you. Ted was that way. Remember, neither one of them came around and drank our booze and stayed up with you until dawn, at which time you'd say, "I don't know about you, but I'm going to bed," and that's how you made out with the younger poets. It was a great technique.

FRANK: It was my work that interested Ted.

JOE: So much so that he was in awe of you. Remember how you used to let him come over and go through your papers to see if he could find some unpublished poems to read? He discovered quite a few, too. But when he wrote that letter, he couldn't have read many of your poems, could he?

FRANK: Just the ones in *Meditations*, I guess, and what Don included in his anthology.

JOE: Didn't he enclose some of his own poems? I think he did.

FRANK: Not in his first letter; he just mentioned that he was a poet. When I wrote back, I asked him to send me some of his stuff.

JOE: I remember wondering if he was gay.

FRANK: You mean you hoped he was.

JOE: Well, I liked his name and the sound of his letters. Then in January 1962, we found out in no uncertain terms that he wasn't.

FRANK: It was a postcard, Joe. He'd written that he was coming to New York in February, and then the weekend we expected him I got this crazy postcard saying that he'd just met a terrific girl named Sandy, and instead of coming to New York he decided to get married. Remember? (JOE *nods*) You know what I can do?

JOE: What?

FRANK: Ask Ted what he remembers about the letter.

JOE: You see him?

FRANK: I haven't run into him yet, but I'm sure I will sometime. I'll look for him.

JOE: Great.

FRANK: (*Rises*) I'll get back to you, Joe. In the meantime, finish typing up what we said today. (*Exits as* JOE *resumes typing, and we fade out*)

—Joe LeSueur

Ted Berrigan Es Muerte

ANDREI CODRESCU

Ted
   un père
if ever there was one
who could fill that place of father
     like no one else
the elephant   the whale
rage of sophisticated life
   so moved by death
Frank's death   Kerouac's death
     elegiac master
impatient with bullshit
    now in their great company
Ted at the crossroads of my youth
  Gem Spa   2nd & St. Mark's
Cajoling threatening kind
   In New York   San Francisco
     Boulder   Baltimore
Délice of repeating what Ted said
   "What did Ted say?"
   "Ted said"
    He said everything
He said that I was the Magellan of sex
    The Bishop of Baltimore
     He said that things were a certain way
and that's the way they were
     after he said them
      forever after
They were and that was that
   Ted in bed
    in the great ship
     going home
Ted who was Mother Courage & Father Bright
  Who kept poetry alive in me
    in people he had not even met

who could say things that he said
& even talk like him
talk in his inimitable way
his widely imitated inimitable way
& I would startle myself saying:
"terrific!" and
"great!"
just as he did
& I heard
my Romanian & someone's Serbian & someone's
French
crossed
by Ted's speech like a wind
crossing the great field of language
to fill it with the seeds
of Ted's heart
his big & wonderful heart!
Generous & direct
amazingly accurate & truthful
knowing   almost always knowing
"what's right"
& amazingly I too knowing
& everyone knowing
The Liberator
who was always "right there"
as he fondly said of someone he admired
Right There! Right There!
Ted you are Right Here
in my heart
"A myth" yes, but more
Your Voice
Farewell, dear teacher, father, poet

— Andrei Codrescu
July 5, 1983

Last Chicago Days

PAUL   HOOVER

In the late seventies, when Ted and Alice announced they were returning to
New York at the end of Ted's fall semester at Northeastern Illinois University
in Chicago, we were all stunned. He had taught there for about five years, but
some sort of dispute had arisen about his M.A. credentials from the University
of Tulsa. He had completed the degree with a thesis on George Bernard Shaw,
but Tulsa wouldn't release his transcript because of some unpaid fees and library
fines. It appeared that Northeastern, in spite of support from fellow faculty
member Alan Bates and others, was trying to give Ted trouble. So he simply
left. We all immediately sensed that an era was ending. The readings at the Body
Politic, many of which were made possible by poets from the coasts being in
town to visit Ted, continued for a while, but without his garrulous presence in
the middle of the second row, commenting on the reader's work with laughs
and asides, the excitement wasn't there. Ted was the Pope of the scene, and he
made everything around him seem important. If Ted praised your work during
or after a reading, you were in heaven, and if he didn't you went home empty.

The week they were leaving town, Art Lange threw a party which
everyone attended. Ted was in terrible shape. His doctor had told him that
if he didn't stop drinking and taking pills he would have only a short time
to live, but he stood at the center of the party, drinking a pint of Southern
Comfort. After each swallow, he would cough deeply and long—a sick
cough. Everyone was worried about him, but we heard he got better in
New York, a city he had missed tremendously. Half of the poetry scene
went with him, including Bob Rosenthal, Shelley Kraut, Simon Schuchat
(whose perfect imitation of Ted's manner of speech always astounded me),
Steve Hamilton and Steve Levine. Later, when Ted won an NEA, word
came that he'd cashed the check at the local currency exchange (the fee was
$350) and walked down the street with money bulging out of his pockets.
We admired the bohemian courage with which Ted and Alice lived at that
time. One visiting poet staying with Ted in Chicago went down to the
kitchen one morning to fix some breakfast, and the only thing he could
find in the cabinets was five bottles of Pernod on a grey shelf.

The next time I saw Ted was when he and Ron Padgett read at Chicago's
Poetry Center. The high point of the visit was a trip to the home of J. Philip
O'Hara, Frank's brother, who lived in a beautiful old white frame house in Oak
Park, Illinois. At the time, Ron was editing a volume of Frank's letters, and he

wanted access to letters in the brother's possession. It was my job to drive Ron and Ted out to the western suburb, where we were greeted by J. Philip with some suspicion. Instead of asking us into the house, he gave us wicker chairs on the porch, where we talked for quite a while on a beautiful June day. He was clearly checking us out, but Ron's business-like manner finally won him over. We were asked to sit inside at the dining room table, onto which O'Hara dumped a shoe box full of Frank's letters and effects. It seemed a gold mine. There were letters from the early sixties from John Ashbery and Edwin Denby, among others. Ashbery's were written on blue airmail stationery from France, and they were full of wit and charm. There was also Frank's passport, issued when he was a curator for the Museum of Modern Art; his employment was given as "Exhibition Specialist." Ted loved this detail and took out his small spiral note pad to write it down. Then he turned to O'Hara's wife, as she passed through the room, to ask if she had any pills. "What sort of pills do you mean," she asked, "aspirin?" "No," said Ted. "Do you have any uppers or speed or anything?" She recoiled as if from a joke, and J. Philip stepped in with the assurance that they didn't have that sort of thing. In fact, Ted had already taken a huge, lethal-looking capsule on the way to Oak Park, and he was probably already high. He proceeded to devour every piece of chocolate candy on the milk-glass dish in the center of the table.

Later, as we were standing to leave, O'Hara asked if we would like to see some of the paintings Frank had owned. He led us to an upstairs bedroom where five or six wonderful paintings by Grace Hartigan, Elaine de Kooning, and others were stacked against the wall. We were in awe. Ted then pointed to the lower right-hand corner of a painting, where a small L-shaped tear had been repaired. " Frank loaned me that painting for about a year," he said, "and it got torn when it fell from my mantel. I gave it back to him like that, but he didn't say anything." We all looked at Ted with amazement, then back at the paintings with increased pleasure. I sensed that J. Philip O'Hara was beginning to appreciate Ted to a small degree; I also felt his sense of relief when he got us out to the car.

I learned of Ted's death four years later while staying on Vinalhaven, an island off the coast of Maine. As we had no phone, the neighbor handed a note in the door to call Richard Friedman and Darlene Pearlstein in Chicago, who gave us the terrible news. I learned on the last day of our stay that the neighbor, Ben Henneke, had been Ted's professor at the University of Tulsa and had followed his career ever since. While we stood on his porch, with the usual fog rolling in, I told him the importance of the note he'd given us.

— Paul Hoover

On Independence Day

ROSE LESNIAK

The messages on my machine
keep repeating the same old thing
"Is he really dead?"
I imagine the open casket
myself kneeling like a saint
and suddenly in the stillness
Ted rises and says,
"Hey, Alice, it worked
How much did we get?"

Poem for Ted

MAXINE CHERNOFF

I'm writing this in verse for you
as Sox are tied at zero, weather gray,
and Koren hates ballet, where mean kids

dance alone. Cheer enters, clumsily,
stage left, when Kenward sends a card
from Weeki Wachi, hokey Florida,

bubbling aquamarine swimmer with an s.o.s.
hello. I wonder if my "this and that" routine
will count. I've always doubted my allure

but maybe what's around me is the theme
told turning to poem. Will it act
interesting as a page of *National Geographic*

featuring Niger's Wodaabe tribesmen, masters
of the sexy glance, who prize male beauty
in the Sahara super-arid desert?

You were sexy, Ted, big hands, cracked voice,
good heart—a tenor, I assume. With teeth
you could have been anything: baseball
commissioner, short-order cook, male lead
in *Tristan and Isolde*. You used to be you,
a beard in bed, the voice in a bad movie.

Like my father you're remembered, October 8,
1983, and it's annoying as a foot asleep,
pink ocean on a map, or a phone call

on vacation telling me you're dead.

The Year in Essex

D O U G L A S   O L I V E R

Many radical students on the uneasy campus of Essex University, England, in 1972 saw all but the most populist poetry as elitist and those who published other kinds came under suspicion of self-advertisement. The unease, left over from "1968," was socially interesting to me; but the wrong-headed notion of poetry bored me no end and I began a give-away duplication service for any student, lecturer or outsider who wanted to publish their work that way. The following year Ted arrived as poet-in-residence, an honorable post whose previous holders had included Ed Dorn and Robert Lowell—the campus had been known for poets ever since Donald Davie was appointed early on as a professor.

Ted's coming pleased me in anticipation: I'd known his work since my years in Cambridge, mid-sixties, and had nearly caught him when I became a sub on the French national news agency in Paris in 1970. George Tysh told me about trying to steer Ted's massive figure, ostentatious joint on lips, down the viciously policed Latin Quarter streets. It's hard to explain to Americans that I was also wary of Ted's coming. He soon asked to see me so that a poetry mag could get started at Essex. Self-educated and wanting to protect my own work against undue American influence, I wasn't necessarily going to help him unless the co-operation between us seemed right. I called in on his office with Simon Pettet, Ralph Hawkins and Charlie Ingham. I had most of the English poetry contacts and he, of course, had the American: I hung back in the conversation until I could be sure I trusted him.

After five minutes of his wonderfully open generosity I had abandoned my tight-lipped Anglo-Scottish reserve and decided I liked him a lot: we also shared a sense of what the campus needed. The mag that we all produced, *The Human Handkerchief,* proved immediately popular, helped to dissolve anti-poetic attitudes on campus, and mixed local with international in just the way I'd hoped.

(Ted had two endearingly different versions of what happened: first, "They didn't know what to do but I showed them," or words to that effect; second, "When I got to Essex, they introduced me to the drug addicts and then to the gays and then I asked, 'Where are the poets?' and they said, 'Well, there's Doug Oliver.'")

It's only recently that I've realized why Ted's year at Essex was so important for him. He made a host of friends, but he made those everywhere; rather, it was a turning point poetically and, with the birth of Edmund at a time very difficult for Alice, the consolidation of their family. The group of poems, *Easter Monday,* the conception of which crystallized in Wivenhoe, the campus village, is where the turning can be studied. Its title poem, influenced by a de Kooning in the Met, has among its assembled voices the phrases, "To go on telling the story" and "A gladness as remote from ecstasy as it is from fear." They indicate that, as after an Easter, the work remained to be done for the rest of his own life whatever the difficulties; the darker times would always be faced with this terrific courage of unemphatic gladness.

At that time, the main work was to broaden his attention internationally: it's no accident that central *Easter Monday* poems typically have international titles. In "So Going Around Cities," the poem that gave its name to his later, major collection, the themes that I'm talking about gather together. It's a poem about the artistic friendliness he prized so much; it has many hints of the tenser aspects of the artistic life; there is an amassing of international reference; the gladness is still paramount with friends toasted in the concluding lines; and its determination to keep faith, to keep telling the story, still captivates me.

As that poem has personal references to myself and Jan, I'll return to Essex reminiscence, 1973-1974, because it will help to explain what I'm saying. Someone's "simplicity" is mentioned in the poem and I imagine it is mine and Jan's, our life together then. The point when our friendship for Ted was finally confirmed came in the New Year, I think, when he called round on us to find my mother, newly a widow, sitting by the gas fire in our Brightlingsea home. Alarmed at his bulk, hairiness, and, to her, bizarre immediacy of friendship, she took refuge, as mothers do, in recalling my childhood. Ted, gleefully realizing that it would please her and, with luck, embarrass me, hugely encouraged her to remember more incidents. Knowing my mother could take it, I all at once weighed in with as many embarrassing anecdotes about my own childhood as I could remember and the joke, never openly stated but shared between the three of us, lifted my mother's spirit and created a bond between me and Ted that never broke.

That year, not least for the links with Ted and Alice, was one of my own most important too. Some of the more vain academics found Ted's style hard to take, though, and I remember telling one of them acidly, "There's a kind of brilliance whose foundation is not academic rationalism but emotional, or intellectual-emotional." I spoke acidly because encountering this other, Berrigan brilliance was becoming my crucial learning experience during the year: "Don't be so tight-arsed."

He had found out quicker than I how to get money out of British arts organizations and, following what had been a lull, a tradition of Essex poetry readings began from the collaboration of all us on *The Human Handkerchief*. As I was broke and my father's death had incurred expense, he arranged a grant for a joint reading and, unexpectedly, handed me his half of the fee. The grant organization didn't know that the gig was actually at his home, the audience our friends; yet it counts as memorable for me. We tailgated, as off the back of the old jazz wagons. He'd say "That's a really mean poem" (English pejorative sense of "mean," I supposed) — and he'd search for something in his own folder to match or to contrast; I'd respond. Another night, in an uncomfortable campus classroom, Alice read with me, her tight, nervy style keeping me on edge.

In the spring Ted brought Anne Waldman to Essex and encouraged Barry Hall to lay on a Harrods- or Fortnum's-catered party at his huge, many-windowed London flat. Dancers turned up from a West End show but the atmosphere was slightly strained because, instead of invited celebrities, there was mainly Ted's student crowd from Essex, who happily wolfed the multi-colored food display.

I look back on that party after all these years and seem to find there Anne breezing through and Ted holding court, as always, while he pretended to dance. As I say, a turning, a moving into the manners of later years, the new darkness of ageing, a holding-on to the value of warmth in the face of hardship. And I honor the poetry from easier times and honor the change itself. He was to have years of financial struggle later and, as the aftermath of hepatitis took its toll, ill-health. "The page has ashes on it," says one of those Essex poems.

But I think of "Work Postures" from that same general period:

> It's hard to fight, when your body is not with you.

& it's equally hard not to. This is the *Easter Monday* spirit that I fell in love with when I met him at Essex, one of the lasting values his friendship has left me.

— Douglas Oliver

Day after Ted Berrigan's Memorial Reading

JOANNE KYGER

Out back
        with Dante looking down his nose, kind of low
        limbed anxiety. Sigh. Don splitting cypress
        from the huge pile felled last winter.
                Is this the form

        I come home to? Yes, and beyond too, oceans
        of paragraphs reiterate the everyday story
        of amazing circumstances in life

        And now the memory is mine
        of your welcoming encouragement,
        greetings at the door, and that
        "Bolinas looks like Korea"
        certainly an exotic touch
        of patience walking thru the streets. Enough!
        I didn't travel
        to the city for words of you but kept it here pretty

well, your picture and some incense — In due respect I was
   so sad now
Dante is in captivity
        the night passed peacefully
      gliding up one current and down
thru another city.

                    August 10, 1983
                    Bolinas

Untitled

JOANNE KYGER

January 12, 1984

        Hello '84

              Ted won't

be in this year. Like dropping in.

    I want

you and I to be

        special in memory's bright clear bobbing flows

    of paper and time.

            I dream

of the worn

        obsidian arrow head found high

    up in lagoon channel cliff side

    where the ground used to be.

Ted Berrigan

BILL BERKSON

I am in love with poetry. Every way I turn,
this, my weakness, smites me.

Ted's walking testimonials were conceived as real-life methods of salvaging what could be identified of amplitude and ethics in the sink of late-middle-century creation. He gave himself steady work as an orator, his poems furthering that sense of toward, from a choice of armchair and street, and snaking back around he'd recombine, he would align so much that was personal with so much he knew was air.

A never-disinterested critic: "I read F as a manual of How to Live." So he took on the plane of the life-language process. (He took the whole fish!)

Ted's advice: "You are having pronoun trouble and I mean only pronoun trouble . . . The obvious solution: Get your own goat."

Some methodology: "I only have two rules actually. Always finish what I start, and never below a certain level." And (advanced creation theory): "There is always a phantasmagoria."

I loved the way when talking/listening his brow would lift and eyeball go convex at the turn of a relevant, unsuspected phrase.

When *The Sonnets* began appearing they seemed to violate a local propriety (other poets, other scenes). They flew over all that, admitting in no secret terms their original smittenness. I felt they were in questionable taste. In 1967 though I got another initiation and the correction thereupon became a permanent pleasure. Ted read those and other poems in the Parish Hall at St. Mark's and our friendship took off then and there.

45. Lewis MacAdams and Ted Berrigan, Boulder, Colorado, 1975. Photo by Rachel Homer.

Big Ted

LEWIS MACADAMS

It's trite,
but the fireworks last night
were the right send-off—Phoebe crying
on the hood of my car as the
rockets glared skyward,
veered & bloomed like you,
you great mountain,
who illumined us both
for two decades then fell
back into the dark.

"red-faced and romping in the wind"

First memory: Colonial Club Lounge, Princeton. Frank O'Hara had agreed to come down to Princeton to do a benefit for my little magazine, *eggs*. O'Hara brought Kenneth Koch, Amiri Baraka (LeRoi Jones then), Joe Brainard, Tony Towle (I think) and Ted Berrigan, who I'd never heard of (1964). I don't remember what Ted read. I was too busy being mortified because only eight people showed up, though the poets didn't seem to mind. At a reception at Colonial Club after the reading, Ted was so excited, enthusiastic, *earnest,* with a totally communicated sense that poetry was the most important activity in the world. First advice to me: get poems for your magazine from some famous poet, then print them on the page facing yours. That way people might read them. He told me to come see him in New York and he'd introduce me to the really great young poets—Gallup and Padgett. He handed me a copy of *"C."* (Robert Wilson at Phoenix Bookshop complaining to me one wintry night not long thereafter after Ted had come in huge and muffled with a slightly unhappy Sandy trying to sell Wilson some paintings she'd done—gouged some few dollars out of Wilson then disappeared into the blowing snow, bell ringing as wooden door slam—Wilson: "I don't know why he prints that magazine on legal-sized paper. Bookstores will never carry them. No one will ever buy them.")

As Usual

Take off your hat & coat & give me all your money
I have to buy some pills and I'm flat broke

Second memory: One of Ted's scams: writing letters to famous author-types asking dozens of searching questions about their work. If they wrote back, Ted'd hustle the missives off to a literary letter buyer of his acquaintance before the gum on the stamps had a chance to dry. Tom Veitch and I on a wintry day with our hands in our pockets stamping our feet to keep warm, standing around with the doorman in front of a lower Fifth Avenue apartment building waiting for Ted to make a deal.

Art: Dutch or Swedish painters staying with Ted and Sandy paid their rent by painting murals of Ted and Sandy in a jovial sex orgy all around the dirty walls of the children's bedroom. I thought it was weird that they painted it, because it seemed that though Ted had wanted it, Sandy hadn't approved.

Little tiny Japanese grandmother sitting beside me on the bus as I write this, eating your grapes and cherries, don't you know my friend is dead, who taught me how to speak?

Lord, it is time. Summer was very great.

Being stunned, one day, for some reason alone at Ted's and for some reason going through the drawers of his desk. Found them full of unpublished manuscripts of his poems: imitation after imitation of Shakespeare, Rimbaud, Rilke, Auden, even Eliot? Realizing Ted's long apprenticeship—that *The Sonnets,* which we (his gang) all knew were momentous even though we (meaning me) could barely understand them, were in some sense the triumph of the student over his academy, or to put it another way, *The Sonnets* were his capture of the fragments gleaned from all his years of study, a triumph, wrestling his homage to his masters into his own statement.

> Going nervously to a drugstore on 14th Street to score speed, spurred on by Ted's "You gonna be one of those guys like Lewis Warsh, who get other people to cop for 'em?" No. Never. Gulp. Ted's big laugh. "Just tell 'em it's for your narcolepsy."

> Ah Bernie, we wear complete
> The indexed Webster Unabridged Dictionary.

I was beginning to understand that the rhetorical, poetical posture of poets, the key that allowed them (us) to spew, or, as Ted put it, turn on the poetry machine, was only a *level.* As perhaps one of the first students of Burroughs with the talent and guts to take him at his word, Ted was slashing through the narrow reality that rhetoric imposed. "You get what I mean there, Dwight?" he would say when I looked dumb. He was laughing but his Scorpio blood was always on fire as Rimbaud's was when he wrote *"J'est un autre."* Although I rarely remember seeing him mad, I remember often thinking that his Scorpio energy and dynamism had the potential to be scary. Sex and death. They were always twined around Ted's long hair like electricity.

> The big green day today is singing to itself
> A vast orange library of dreams.

> It is a human universe: & I
> is a correspondent.

He was caught in a big, thick body. His identification with Kerouac starts with the sense that they were both New Englanders and both brought up poor. Like Kerouac, Ted had scorn for and hated his body. In their *Paris Review* interview, Kerouac told Ted to get his teeth fixed. Ted never did. And bad teeth seemed to be an excuse for his famous, rotten diet of peanut butter sandwiches and Pepsi . . .

> this poem upon the page
> will not kneel   for everything comes to it
> gratuitously.

For the first time I'm beginning to understand the materiality of his words, objectifying them for use ("massive as Anne's thighs upon the page") over and over in *The Sonnets,* so that one saw language as solid, reflectant. "The logic of grammar is not genuine." The same phrase reflecting a different meaning in a different place in the poems. ("belly to hot belly/we have lain.")

"The poems" is not a dream for all things come to them.

Learning from Ted about integrity — that to be a poet, if you do it well, is *enough,* despite the poverty, the sickness, the loss . . . "my dream a crumpled horn."

But for God's sake, is there anyone out there listening?

For me the supreme works were in 1963, 1964, 1965. "Words for Love," the great last stanza turning John Wieners' "Poem for Painters" over on its head, *Tambourine Life,* the "Personal Poems."

It's funny how much difference time can make on inflection. How the same sentence, once funny, can later turn ironic then still later sad, without ever leaving the page.

"For God's sake, is there anyone out there listening?" in "Living with Chris" brought a big laugh the first time I heard it, but now . . . ?

> you'd be surprised, however
> at how much difference
> a really good cup of coffee and a few pills can make.

As the pills began to take over his life, the poems began to proclaim something more than the man Ted Berrigan. He began to be Ted Berrigan, the character in his poems — bad teeth, jangled nerves, long hair and beard flaked with ashes from his non-filter cigarettes, Pall Malls, Chesterfield Kings and,

46. Frontispiece for *Tambourine Life,* by Bobbie Louise Hawkins. Published by Mother Press, 1965.

after living in England, Senior Service. Sleeping all day, working all night, throwing on his Jim Bridger jacket at dawn to go for Pepsi and the papers at Gem Spa. Was this Ted, or was he the Ted in the poems, the bridge to the legendary poet he was creating out of his life? Whitman's legitimate son, a child of the Lower East Side where, for me, he and Ed Sanders divided up the beatnik power. Ted even wrote a song for Ed to sing, one of the early Fugs' hits. "I don't want to go to Vietnam. I want to stay right here and screw your Mom . . . People see me on the street they yell Jesus Christ! But I'm getting mine, I'm doing all right."

Ted held court most often at 33 St. Mark's Place where Anne Waldman lived with Lewis Warsh after she'd graduated from Bennington, and later when she lived there with Michael Brownstein. At 33 St. Mark's Ted seemed like a visiting king. Anne worked while her men grumbled and argued, or acted amused and tried to wedge themselves a place on the couch. No doubt one reason he was always there was because of his increasingly fractured marriage. At the same time (late '60s) a few teaching jobs began coming his way. First in Iowa, where his marriage finally came apart, then Michigan.

> Is there room in the room that you room in?

> It's 5 below zero in Iowa City tonight.

> This year I found a warm room
> that I could go to
>   be alone in
> & never have to fight.

> I didn't live in it.

I hitchhiked to Iowa City once from San Francisco to pay a visit. It was the first time I ever saw Ted really sad, living in a room where he wouldn't answer the door. On that same trip I first met Alice Notley, pale, willowy, intense—who was beginning to meet Ted in coffee shops while being followed around by one of Ted's subalterns, a maniac named Henry Pritchett.

> and between these two passages (from
> the long poem "Biotherm") occurs a me-
> diating line which might stand to charac-
> terize all of Mr. O'Hara's art:
> "I am guarding it from mess and message."
>   ★

WATERLOO SUNSET

Nature makes my teeth "to hurt"

Cold rosy dawn in New York City
                                    not for me

Sometime near the end of the psychedelic era, friends started leaving New York for the West Coast. Ted, who considered the Lower East Side his turf, got beat up by a gang of kids in Tompkins Square Park and broke his leg. He began to refer to himself as the elephant and started talking about losing weight. Jim Carroll came along like Ted's kid brother, and suddenly there was another generation. New York began to mean less and less. Ted and Alice arrived in Bolinas to live in a (barely) converted garage behind my & Phoebe's & baby Ocean Lee's house overlooking Duxbury Point (circa 1971). They were absolutely penniless and used every available cent for speed. Alice weighed about eighty pounds. Ted slept and wrote and came out only at night to wander down to Smiley's Bar, shoot pool and hang out.

Ted didn't like what he saw in Bolinas — poets working as plumbers, painters workings as carpenters, etc. He thought it infantile and a misuse of talent. To my insistence that we were part of a new society in which everyone would have to do everything for themselves, Ted would respond with long, bombastically accurate letters and proclamations that writing poetry well was enough. "It takes your best shot," he wrote, "to do whatever." Tom Clark, who refused to have anything to do with anybody or anything but his poetry, his pot, his woodpile and his family, pleased Ted the most. At Christmas, Ted wrote Phoebe and me each a long letter telling us what kind of present to buy ourselves in his name. He pushed us to read Mother Goose and Ruth Krauss ("Hope You Happy, Monkey") to the kid, and not "that baboon, Dr. Seuss."

          30

     The fucking enemy shows up

Ted's work began moving more and more towards death. In fact, he became Kerouac's partner in the ongoing hymn to death they both whistled all the way to their graves. "Memorial Day" opened the door, or more accurately, began to close the door behind him.

My friends whose deaths have slowed my heart stay
with me now.

I rarely saw him in the late seventies. When I did, his monomania and his preaching became so weary to me that I never knew what to do. Smiling, leaving his and Alice's and the kids' shotgun apartment with my head down. My last memories, St. Mark's Place late at night early in the 1980s, a crowd of weary listeners edging away from Ted as he talked. He didn't even acknowledge they were gone.

TELEGRAM
        to Jack Kerouac

Bye-Bye Jack.
See you soon.

One wants to sum up in a way that means something. I can think of a dozen situations—stealing books, talking about basketball. One day we agreed to start a collaboration over the telephone. He started writing as I hung up. I started writing as I left the apartment I was staying at and caught a bus to 14th Street where he and Donna Dennis were living in Rudy Burckhardt's loft. We wrote together all afternoon. Ted at Warhol's Factory with the Brillo Box that Andy gave him. Ted pontificating all over the U.S. . . . Ted of Battersea. Ted's last days at Naropa, ill. Ted saying "Totally Great." That's when I want to stop. When he was filled with joy. "Not ecstasy," he cautioned once, "joy." That's how I like to think of Ted, Pepsi in hand, army pants, lumberjack shirt on, orating. "Totally great," I can hear him saying. I still feel great when I hear him saying it out loud, right now, in eternity, "Totally Great!"

—Lewis MacAdams

Conversation with Ted (made-up)

JACK COLLOM

Hi Ted.

Hi Jack. I'm just finishing this story. So he said, my heart is broken. And I said, don't bet on it. Alice, where's my pants? I used to see W. H. Auden at this deli on 5th Street. He led the chemical life. One day he was standing there trying to eat a hot dog, spilling mustard all over the floor, talking about this asthmatic boyfriend of his who breathed like a dog. He looked terrific, like a walnut. Uppers for breakfast, a glass of brandy late morning, some hash after supper, snort a little coke and take a bottle of wine to bed. How're you doing? Ten years ago you looked a little blue in the left hand. I'm going uptown to sell some books. Can you lend me eight cents for a cab? Alice, what do we need besides Pepsi and macaroni? Toilet paper. Here's my new book. You'll notice I'm not even in it. Let Eddie have that crocodile awhile, Anselm. Ron and I used to worry about the problem of continuity in poetry until we finally figured out when you say something, say something else. So long.

April 18, 1982

4 Ted

SIMON PETTET

O wait a minute, there's something in my eye no,
Wait it is an eyeball, no wait, there are
Two of them, and they are, looking at you but they are not
Regretful, o no they are not, and they are not sad, no,
Tho' he is no longer among us, and we so dearly loved
—and still love—him.

47. Ted Berrigan at 101 St. Mark's Place, New York City, 1982. Photo by Mark Hillringhouse.

Canzone

for Ted Berrigan, 1934-1983

ANNE WALDMAN

I crisscross my feelings with a view
of street, people walking, some crazy looking, from a window
Some could be anyone, me, you, Ted, with your own "view"
Could anyone else share? Tinted clouds today. His view
Which some thought extreme, distorted, stubborn,
making friends into Myth where they became viewed
with excessive scrutiny & magnified into situations in
        which only the Heavens dare intervene
He said, Propitiate the gods! They love to intervene
as you walk, sleep, talk, make love, drink soda in plain view
of them. I'll put in a good word, you show-offs! I have long talks

with them at night about you, no evasions when the muses talk
This was the energy Ted sought by talk

As if there were no other way close enough to get a multiple view of self, and
tell some history through layers of talk
He would tell his heart to talk
& it did & enlarged the domains of art, his mind was behind a window
out of which he could throw propriety, then remake language,
        steal it from books, from fast elegant talk
to discover the power that lives in printed words & talk
is captive, you can re-invent the world, it's not so stubborn
about bringing poems into focus. Huddle, team, to talk
Ted lying before his audience in bed, a practiced man, his memory then
        intervene
fundamental to the thing seen, the thing thought, then Death could
        intervene

Pugnacious, subversive, president of the adventure, Death intervened
to taste & magnify the ingredients, but also end talk
although I hear it still go on. Mysterious noises intervene
to shake the poet out of her sleep to recognize his cargo, & to intervene
on behalf of Ted who won't ever formulate a neat view
Here is a non-utilitarian cigarette, but it can't intervene
between us anymore, it won't intervene
as you once flicked ash on my lap (I was indignant), then out the window
Or you once beheld all of Boston from my airplane window
Did you ever belong to me? Could I never intervene
to make you healthier, less quivering with stubborn
love or pride? I loved you of course for being stubborn

You were inhabiting the same stubborn
poems as I was. I can't look out the window
without missing you without being angry at you, stubborn
in a kind of grief that won't let me write now, head stubborn
& the typewriter waiting for a new oracle who will talk
vast magical ruminations spelled out from the moment, sing of a stubborn
time insistent upon war for chatter for stubborn stammerings
to make life more exalted, a point of view

which uses dreams because they are my imagination my view
now of you as a full citizen of this country no matter how stubborn
I breathe in the colors from the window
I stand in the early morning light of the window

Are you drawn back to look in my window?
If so, I'll be capacious, I want to ask you something stubborn
"I am a bountiful cotton crop" you wrote on your last postcard window
like a cartoon. Then my name and address: "Mt. Olympus,
        Near Bo-Tree, Manhattan." You drew an octagon window
Your handwriting makes me laugh, it would always intervene
optimistically. Did you mean to keep me in the picture? The window
is shut, I went away, a stranger moved into the apartment,
        no need to shout up at the window
I miss your comparisons, prodigious talk
We are as unlike as people can be in our talk
It is 1967. You call up at the window
with your rotund ambition, a cosmopolitan view
Let's get high, let's fall in love, let's ride uptown & see
what the painters are doing with a view

Is it nothing more than strange antics, a view
I'll never own, nor you, nor greater intensity than talk
will ever do, when grief does spill over & intervene to the present?
My equilibrium is swaying as the 20th century stubbornly shuts down
I was there & I was there by the window onto you.

— Anne Waldman
33 St. Mark's Place
November 1983

48. Alice Notley and Ted Berrigan reading together at the Beat 'n' Path Cafe, Hoboken, New Jersey, December 10, 1980. Photo by Pietro Gigli.

On a Poet

DAVID SHAPIRO

Wallace Stevens once shocked a friend by attending a party for Carl Sandburg and making the request that Archibald MacLeish *not* be invited. Sandburg had, for Stevens, a certain reality. Then there is a poet who asks that everyone be invited.

Differences among poets sometimes seem to be everything. But Stevens is also correct, after making differentiations in *The Necessary Angel* between poets who have something to say of modern sense and poets who are concerned mostly with the form of what they say, that there is a resemblance between poets of imagination and those of reality. Then there is a poet who would laugh at these words.

Between me and Ted Berrigan there often seemed to exist a gulf fixed as between imagination and reality. I have come to respect that part of him that was involved entirely in responding to the pressure of what seemed a new reality, whether it was a precise locale or moment or momentum. I think thinking for him was very much a matter of the faculties of perception, and this finally is not so different than the asceticism I sometimes prefer in the thinking that would like to escape or deny place and the natural or made-up clock. What matters, Stevens says, is the opposition to poetry of contempt or trivia. Ted felt, with Stevens, that poetry was vital and experimental. That is why there are more connections between the poetry of say Berrigan and Ashbery than between that of Berrigan and many of his so-called disciples or friends. The influence of a poet of reality such as Ted may easily become a false pressure, because what is generated is a taste for local detail and time that has none of his vital conflicts. But that is beside the point of his essential value, an authenticity that attracted an austere temperament such as Fairfield Porter to his work.

Berrigan's best work has a pathos and a method. The pathos and method inspired two painters of "homeless representation": Jim Dine and Jasper Johns. I recall Dine particularly remarking on a poem that includes a fierce rapprochement between a son and a mother. The poet discovers that his mother too has had a certain freedom and conceived him before her marriage. The son comes to a reconciliation with forms of the middle-class that he elsewhere may seem too easily to defy or disdain. When Berrigan chose to parody one of my early poems entitled "We Are Gentle," he chose to make a sound-translation of it as "We Are Jungles," but the parody was less caustic than Ron Padgett's "We Are Gentiles," because Ted always admitted to a taste for the sentimental. He always appreciated appreciation and never felt more uneasy than with certain forms of analysis. He loved positive analysis. He had loved Conrad Aiken's worst poems — the anthology pieces — and maintained a comical balance in his work between a freshness caught at the expense of an out moded lyricism and a music that could seem all too mellifluous.

I think that some of his best poetry was informed by his dissonant experiences during the Korean War. He once told me that upon his release from the army he experienced every street or site as a place that had to be held, militarily. He laughed at trauma and reminds us of Apollinaire's happy dictum, "I can die and smile as well." He told me that Eisenhower had visited Joyce's tower and said nothing but, "With two guns I could control that bay." He was capable of loving Strangelove. I think that the trauma of the war is often overlooked in relation to those who fought in it. It was not a just war and was not thought of as such. I think that at least part of Berrigan's experiences in such a war influenced his lack of response to convention or his wild distaste for it. These experiences he often joked about. I admired his army poem, "Corporal Pellegrini" and he dedicated it to me/in one version. Ted was the antithesis of the bureaucrat, and bureaucracy is one or perhaps the chief enemy of art and life in our time.

Stevens, whom I have been quoting too much here, talked once of the sadness of the death of little magazines and that they of course constituted the best of what could be read in America. I think that it is easy to overlook the fact that Berrigan, with almost no resources except generosity and devotion, undertook to print what he considered to be the best poets of his time in a magazine named comically after the comedian as letter *C,* and that these poets may have seemed once a sort of squad, coterie, of friendly soldiers, but have become, after all, history: Ashbery, Schuyler, Burroughs, Koch, Denby, Ceravolo. Berrigan's role as an editor is very impressive. This is probably more significant than his explicit collaborations with other poets and was, perhaps, his best collaboration. Even though we were both moved by disdain for the other's conventionality or conventional lack of it, both of us were involved in a collaboration of a kind and knew it. I was moved when he visited my family in Newark, New Jersey, talked to my older sister at great length, and paid attention to my father's sculpture. He printed more of my poems in his magazine than I expected and he always asked for more. We fought in England once over matters of taste and he remarked to me that I was not going to stop his particular brand of self-destructiveness, which sometimes terrified me. His vocal support and cheerfulness were significant to me as to many; for example, I have kept a really hearty postcard upon the publication of my first book.

I had met Ted in 1964 at the Wagner Writer's Conference, the second and last I attended. He often played the role of a summer savage from Oklahoma, then would speak didactically about his love for Shaw and Whitehead. I remember remarks on poetry, as when he commented to someone that he would revise a line of mine about being on a beach to being on a beach ball. I remember his immense magnaminity toward Joe Ceravolo, an entirely different kind of poet whom he featured again and again in his magazine. I loved Joe's Reverdy-like purity and admired Ted's admiration for it. Ted also dazzled me by his sudden academicism of collecting every scrap of Ashbery and F. T. Prince. For all of his boldness, this editorial devotion seemed student-like and paradoxically demure.

One of our last meetings was with his wife and children and Johnny Stanton. They had been caught in a downpour at Columbia University and visited us while laughing and dripping. Johnny drove us in a frightening truck in careening rain to inexpensive hamburgers in Queens. I remember being struck by Ted's authoritative replies to his wife about poetry. He commanded and liked to command. Since I didn't trust him academically, I was always very cautious about his charisma, but it was there. Like anyone else, I recall the strength of his laughter and his peculiarly witty way of using superlatives for anything.

When I think of Ted, I think of the fact that one of my favorite putative lines of O'Hara was written by him ("feminine marvelous and tough") in an extraordinary homage. I think, too, of the humility of his best poems, that he was willing to caricature and characterize himself as a creature among toilet papers and typewriters and pills, and also that there is in him, in a highly developed state, the theme of friendship even more than romantic love. His best poems may be the one in which he speaks of being "alight with borrowed warmth" from a friend's jacket on a cold night. Waley said the West had exaggerated the theme of love, and friendship had become a topic and style in O'Hara's poetry, but in a way Ted was more obviously "genial" than Frank ever was. Frank and Ted however reveal the true insomnia and pathos of those whose friendships are necessary because of the terror of isolation. Therefore, I do not find their social poems, so-called, any more or less heart breaking than poems of a more obvious isolation.

I think Ted in his *Sonnets* — that are often extremely dissolute in appearance and influence — created some cardboard cutouts that are as chaste and fine and humble as anything in the Arte Povera movement that followed Pop Art. Ted might have regarded the whole conceptual movement as a joke that he could have turned into a fiction: a movement signed by one author. In a sense, Ted's poetry wove between the poles of a fullness of content and a taste for the humiliations of experiment. His work is both at the origin of a literary equivalent of "Pop" art and leads by way of extreme prosiness and collage to a kind of conceptual bareness, not "I do this, I do that," but a list of "what to do." His use of serial form, admired by Johns, has not been made use enough of in poetry and is extremely provocative. It reminds one of the remark of Valéry that one should print a poem of all the variations of that poem. Ted was lead to a new Whitmanian idea of almost infinite materialistic variation and inclusivity that went along with what was most positive in his character. Because he included, he was a poet. When he died, I recalled the simplicity of his advice, to a student friend, that when writing the word "love," one should always comically try its opposite, and then learn something about ambivalence. Ted taught about whimsical methods that led to serious truths. He never gave up his seriousness or his sensuousness.

Claims made on behalf of Ted and his poetry often seem extravagant or unreasonable because he made such minimal claims himself. It's more true of him than anyone that he had a repugnance for false nobility, such as—in this very essay—the diction I am using. So democratic was he in his praise and so catholic in his taste that it is hard not to be democratic and simply place him as part of a circle whose circumference is everywhere. But actually tolerance and flexibility and the democratic are qualities not so easily arrived at and Ted's poetry has not been reproduced so easily. He was one of the destroyers of an old hierarchy and made room for a new pluralism. The fate of such pluralism is to become an excuse for permissiveness, a permission that is actually at odds with the man who stayed up every night to write sonnets with permutations from the masters he adored, derided and revitalized.

When a famous poet "goosed" him, he said, "If you do that again, I'll kill you." To which the poet, a friend, responded, "And you're just the person who would." His good humor may be seen in a wild parody of a letter of rejection that he wrote one of my high school classmates who had submitted poems to his magazine. His self-characterizations in it are funny, sad and precise. Ted wanted this brief primary-colored life and has written that he would resent anyone who didn't understand that. His lack of dissociation killed him in an age requiring more narrow medicine than courage and poetry.

—David Shapiro

Drysdale and Mantle, Whitey Ford and to You

STEVE CAREY

Wet snow falling on no snow
Go on over and ask her to dance
then we'll toast the old bastards
and shut this gathering up

There is precious little
between bites
but it is hard to lightly bite
loved ones
for thinking of dead ones

That man's joy, that woman's joy
comes to us
not so much in similar words
—quote or coincidence—
but I think in lethal duet
vowel train, crossword puzzle whim
—a flick of the scat-capable wig

The man I am thinking about
is—good God—hereabouts

and this is the Last Call he heard
from the day he was born—O Ted!

Copy Legends with Ted Berrigan

GERARD MALANGA

4:vii:83 nyc
Ted,
tell me
what it's
like
on the other side.

Tell me
what time
it is.

49. Ted Berrigan at Gem Spa, St. Mark's Place and 2nd Ave, 1971. Photo by Gerard Malanga.

50. Ted Berrigan encounters John Ashbery in front of the St. Regis Hotel, 1971. Photo by Gerard Malanga.

51. Ted Berrigan and Ted Greenwald in the courtyard of St. Mark's Church In-the-Bowery, 1971. Photo by Gerard Malanga.

52. Anne Waldman, Ted Berrigan and Bernadette Mayer at a party for Ted given by Victor Bockris and Bobbi Bristol at their flat, 1974. Photo by Gerard Malanga.

53. Ron Padgett and Ted Berrigan at The Poetry Project, 1978. Photo by Gerard Malanga.

54. René Ricard, Ted Berrigan and Reed Bye at The Poetry Project, 1978. Photo by Gerard Malanga.

55. Ted Berrigan, Kathy Acker and Johnny Stanton outside One University Place Restaurant, 1980. Photo by Gerard Malanga.

56. Ted and Kate Berrigan, corner of 8th Street and Broadway, just a few days before Ted's death, 1983. Photo by Gerard Malanga.

For Ted

ED SANDERS

We were both using the same
mimeo machine
at the Phoenix Bookshop
in 1963
you for "C" magazine
I for "Fuck You/A Magazine of the Arts"

It was obvious
we were slaves
to the lyre and the bee

& we wanted a better
performance
out of our soma

We pranced around
our mimeo machines
like Bassarids

the benzene dripping
from our fingers

& the foxskins
        masking our smiles

You were one of the first
guys
(you and Blackburn)
I met
who lived it
around the clock
and now you're gone
gone too early

and it doesn't matter
now how
we twisted our guts
in the face of the
creator.

Later you ran a series of readings
at the Café Le Metro down the
Street from the St. Mark's Church
and printed some of your flyers
at the Peace Eye Bookstore
such as the one you wrote for
May 19th 1965:

"JEROME ROTHENBERG
Everybody knows Jerry. His latest book,
SIGHTINGS, cracks the windows of the eyes
with its sonic silence. Better harden yr
heart for this reading"

and this: "MINIMUM 25 cents."

You worked your body
for almost half a century
as if you were a vaulter
before a leap

We were combative. We fought
about an issue so stupid it's a blush
to recall.

Maybe this is too personal &
packed with the capital I
to publish
for it's you I want to celebrate.

But I feel a grinding
in my soul.

It's an evil
        economic system
that does not
take care of poets.

Sometimes the sky
            drips curses
Sometimes the sky
            drips glee

But a country with a
rotten economy drips
bad times
            for bards

You told me George Kimball
asked you once to a Red Sox game
but that you couldn't go
not owning the proper clothes

It is an
utter &
complete disgrace
that there was
no free national
health system
to which you could
have consulted
        readily
            & easily

America, where bad
teeth cost as much
as a Honda

where poverty
the curse of Chatterton
& Edmund Spenser

still eats
the marrow
        of poets.

I recall the weeping
on the outdoor concrete platform
the echoing gukh's
like standing in a cistern

and your daughter Kate
        with striking red hair
her beautiful face
            shining with tears
walked up to place
a single white rose
            on the coffin.

                        —Ed Sanders

Ted Berrigan's Published Work: A Checklist

A Lily for My Love. (Providence: Privately published, 1959), wrappers.

The Sonnets. (New York: Lorenz and Ellen Gude, 1964), wrappers, 300 numbered copies. Cover by Joe Brainard.

Seventeen. (New York: Privately published, Ted Berrigan & Ron Padgett, 1964), 100 copies. Note: With Ron Padgett.

A Newbaby Was Born. (n.p.: Privately published, 1965), broadside. Note: Birth announcement collage.

Living with Chris. (New York: Boke Press, 1965), wrappers. Drawings by Joe Brainard.

The Sonnets. (2nd Edition: New York: Grove Press, 1966).

Some Things. (n.p., CA: 1966), mimeographed sheet in folder. Note: With Ron Padgett.

Bean Spasms. (New York: Kulchur Press, 1967), two issues, no priority: 1.) hardcover, acetate dustwrapper 2.) wrappers. Note: With Ron Padgett. Drawings by Joe Brainard.

Many Happy Returns. (New York: Angel Hair, 1967), single poem, self–wrappers, no priority: 1.) 200 copies 2.) 4 copies, lettered, signed by the author.

Many Happy Returns. (New York: Corinth Books, 1969), wrappers, no priority: 1.) 1450 copies 2.) 50 copies, numbered, signed by the author and illustrator. Cover by Joe Brainard.

Doubletalk. (Iowa City: Privately published, 1969), wrappers, 240 copies, signed by the authors. Note: With Anselm Hollo.

Peace. (Detroit: Alternative Press, 1969), broadside.

NOH. (n.p.: Lines Press, 1969), broadside, 50 copies, numbered, signed by the authors. Linesheet 1.) Note: With Ron Padgett.

A Fragment. (London: Cape Goliard Press, 1969), broadside in folder, no priority: 1.) 267 copies, numbered 2.) 60 copies, numbered, signed by the author and illustrator. Illustrated by Jim Dine.

Scorpion, Eagle & Dove. (n.p.: Privately published, 1970), broadside, no priority: 1.) Trade Edition 2.) 50 copies, numbered, signed by the author.

In the Early Morning Rain. (London: Cape Goliard Press, 1970), hardcover, no priority: 1.) Trade Edition 2.) 100 copies, numbered, signed by the author. Cover by George Schneeman.

Poems, In Brief. (Bolinas, CA: Privately published, 1971), wrappers, manila folder, 12 copies, numbered, signed by the author. Note: Comprises the only issue of *The Synthetic Magazine.*

Memorial Day. (New York: Poetry Project, St. Mark's Church In-the-Bowery, 1971), wrappers. Note: With Anne Waldman. Cover by Donna Dennis.

Train Ride. (New York: Vehicle Editions, © 1971 but published much later), 1,500 copies. Cover by Joe Brainard.

Memorial Day. (London: Aloes Books, 1972), wrappers. Note: With Anne Waldman.

Back in Boston Again. (New York: Telegraph Books, 1972), wrappers, no priority: 1.) Trade Edition 2.) 50 copies, numbered, signed by the authors. Note: With Tom Clark and Ron Padgett.

Vort #2. (Spencer, IN: 1972) Note: This is a Ted Berrigan/Anselm Hollo number of this magazine.

The Drunken Boat. (New York: Adventures In Poetry, 1974), wrappers. Drawings by Joe Brainard.

A Feeling for Leaving. (New York: Frontward Books, 1975), wrappers, no priority: 1.) 375 copies 2.) 25 copies, numbered, signed by the author 3.) 3 copies, hors commerce. Cover by Rochelle Kraut.

Red Wagon. (Chicago: Yellow Press, 1976) Cover by Rochelle Kraut.

Clear the Range. (New York: Adventures In Poetry/Coach House South, 1977), wrappers, 750 copies. Covers by Ted Berrigan and George Schneeman.

Nothing for You. (Lenox, MA & NY: Angel Hair Books, 1977), 1000 copies. Cover and frontispiece by George Schneeman.

Yo-Yo's with Money. (Henniker, NH: United Artists Books, 1979), wrappers, 500 copies. Cover by Rosina Kuhn.

Carrying a Torch. (Brooklyn, NY: 1980), 500 copies. Note: This is issue #22 of *Clown War.*

So Going Around Cities: New & Selected Poems 1958-1979. (Berkeley: Blue Wind Press, 1980) Cover reproduction of painting by Donna Dennis. Drawings by George Schneeman.

In a Blue River. (New York: Little Light, 1981), 500 copies. Cover by Susan Cataldo.

The Sonnets.(3rd Edition: New York: United Artists, 1982) Covers by Louise Hamlin. Frontispiece by Joe Brainard. Note: 6 sonnets omitted from the original manuscript were restored for this edition.

A Certain Slant of Sunlight. (Oakland, CA: O Books, 1988). Front cover reproduction of postcard by Ted Berrigan and Joanne Kyger. Cover design by publisher, Leslie Scalapino. Note: Includes reproductions of some of the postcards Ted made and wrote for The Alternative Press series.

IN TRANSLATION:

Guillaume Apollinaire Ist Tot. (Frankfurt, Germany: Marz Verlag, 1970), wrappers, dustwrapper. Note: Bilingual edition with photographs, and drawings by Joe Brainard and George Schneeman.

Compiled by Anne Waldman

Index

Clark, Tom
24, 42, 64-65, 74-85, 129-130, 216

Clown War
243

Codrescu, Andrei
150, 198-199

Cohen, Marvin
93-94

Cohn, Jim
104-115

Collaboration
52, 75, 116, 118, 162, 190,
206, 217, 225, 242-244

Collom, Jack
218

Columbia University
9, 125, 225

Coolidge, Clark
15, 48, 98-101, 105

Corinth Books
242

Craig, Andrea
111

Crabtree, Lee
63, 67

Creeley, Robert
20-24, 71, 85, 104-105, 108, 128, 136

Cubism
48-50, 113

D

Dada
28, 33

Davie, Donald
204

Dawson, Fielding
65

de Kooning, Elaine
201

de Kooning, Willem
10, 42-43, 49, 205

Denby, Edwin
41, 43, 79, 177, 201, 225

Dennis, Donna
42, 46-59, 217, 243

Dine, Jim
224, 242

di Prima, Diane
106-107

Dorn, Edward
104-107, 136, 178, 204

Drugs
VIII, 27-36, 42, 48-54, 65-66, 69, 75,
88, 112, 114-115, 140, 142, 144, 148-152,
156, 162-163, 173, 179, 200-201, 204,
212-213, 216, 218, 226

Duchamp, Marcel
10, 18, 52, 109

Duncan, Robert
12-14, 84, 104-107

E

Einstein, Albert
5

Eliot, T. S.
43, 75, 110, 212

Elmslie, Kenward
44, 47, 69, 86, 144, 150, 203

Eshleman, Clayton
31

Essex University
VII, 148-149, 204-206

F

Fagin, Larry
41-43, 52, 68

Foster, Ed
99

Fraser, Kathleen
107, 135

Friedman, Richard
201

1.16.93 MIDWEST H+G 93072